HELP YOURSELF!

... a Story of FBI Corruption

——— by ———

Martin L. Kaiser III

Robert S. Stokes, Editor

www.trafford.com
North America & international
toll-free: 844-688-6899 (USA & Canada)
fax: 812 355 4082

I will be as harsh as the truth and uncompromising as justice.[1]

William Lloyd Garrison (1805—1879)

---

[1] William Lloyd Garrison, "To the Public," Fair Use Repository, accessed September 9, 2024, https://fair-use.org/the-liberator/1831/01/01/the-liberator-01-01.pdf.

CONTENTS

CONTENTS

FOREWORD

Marty Kaiser grew up in a blue-collar working family in Northeastern Pennsylvania. He was the typical patriotic American with a love for his country and a dream to someday make a difference. He was to become the United States government's top technical eavesdropping spymaster. He could craft a "bug," or listening device, no one could find, or build a system that would detect devices planted by foreign governments.

Marty's US government clients for surveillance and countersurveillance equipment included the who's who of the three-letter covert US intelligence agencies. He was the equivalent of "Agent Q" in the British James Bond movies.

Marty Kaiser is also a man of ethics and integrity. When called to testify before the House Select Committee on Intelligence regarding the FBI's purchasing procedures, he simply told the truth in an effort to assist the Committee with its investigation. That testimony would place him on a collision course with internal FBI corruption at the highest levels and make him the target of shocking retribution.

Because of his mastery of technical eavesdropping, Marty was recruited by Walt Disney Productions/Touchstone Pictures to provide technical support for the surveillance devices portrayed in the movie *Enemy of the State*. The film is an excellent portrayal of the power of government secrecy and surveillance, and the consequences of its abuse. How ironic it is that the theme of the film would be played out in real life with the advent of the NSA domestic spy program, which secretly arose out of the unbridled US Patriot Act. NSA surveillance of innocent US citizens would indeed become a reality. The FBI would begin secret, warrantless searches of American homes and businesses. The CIA would operate secret prisons worldwide under horrific conditions. All this would be done *without constitutional validation.*

Help Yourself!...A Story of FBI Corruption is a fascinating, uncensored, and refreshingly candid story of a man who rose to be considered the US government's top expert on eavesdropping. It is the story of a man who went up against the Goliath of government corruption alone, and paid the price for refusing to back down from the truth. *Help Yourself!...A Story of FBI Corruption* is the story of how a government can become alarmingly corrupted by the abuse of secrecy and the addiction to the power of its agents. These agents attempted to destroy the business, reputation, and family of a true American patriot who wanted to serve his country. In Marty Kaiser's case, they messed with the wrong man.

Kevin M. Shipp,
Former CIA Officer
Author of *From the Company of Shadow: CIA Secrecy and Operations* and *Twilight of the Shadow Government.*

PROLOGUE

Now that my autobiography, *Odyssey of an Eavesdropper* is published and available worldwide in hardcover, paperback, and Kindle, it is time to move on to my memoirs. Come join me in a journey through my life.

Born 1935 in Wilkes-Barre, Pennsylvania, I lived with my two brothers, Al and Ron, and parents in one-half of a duplex house on Horton Street. It was a basic house consisting of a living/dining room, kitchen, three bedrooms, and one bathroom. The kitchen stove and furnace were both coal-fired. Dad was a plumber who worked for his father, owner of Martin L. Kaiser Company, Plumbing and Heating. My grandfather worked for his father, my great-grandfather, who emigrated from Prussia in 1858. He served in the Civil War, rising to a rank of sergeant. The Kaiser copper and tinsmith business began in Prussia and can be traced to the late 1700s.

My very early years consisted primarily of playing in the backyard sandbox or swinging on the swing. On rainy days, I played on the dirt portion of the cellar floor. Eventually, my boundary was extended to my best friend Charlie Siegel's yard two houses away, where Charlie and I spent hours hanging out in his cherry tree thinking up games to play. One memory, in particular, remains frozen in my head, literally. At age four, I was sitting at the kitchen table when we heard the drone of a multiengine aircraft. We all ran outside and there was a *huge* zeppelin about one thousand feet overhead. Each of the six engines had a gondola from which the passengers could view the activity below and wave their handkerchiefs. Not watching, I lost my footing, fell off the fourth step, and cracked my skull on the sidewalk below. I still remember my father holding me on the doctor's table while the doctor stitched me up. During the war, I would use my Radio Flyer wagon to collect tin cans for the war effort. A stamp was given for each wagonload. That stamp was then stuck on a card that represented the weapon I was buying. Mine was a tank.

The railroad tracks were roughly one hundred yards from our house. Whenever Mom would hear a locomotive passing nearby, she would rush outside to gather up the laundry before the "clinkers" (ash) fell on the clothes. Eventually, I was permitted to go as far as the railroad trestle. I was always awestruck by the size of the steam locomotives, their sound, and the one hundred plus cars full of sparkling diamonds of coal they were hauling. Once in a while, a hobo would jump from one of the cars; sometimes, hobos would show up at our kitchen door, with hats in hand, asking for something to eat.

Mom always had a sandwich and drink for them. I admired Mom for her caring.

The uneven flagstone sidewalk made roller-skating a real challenge. Around age six, I began building airplane models, usually hiding in the closet at night to finish a project. I'm lucky I did not asphyxiate myself from the glue I was using. A few years later, Dad gave me a gasoline powered "U-control" model airplane. The OK29 engine used a spark plug along with its associated coil, points, and spark advance lever. That's me in the picture second from the left at the local airplane club. After a few crashes and a lot of broken propellers, I was finally able to keep the plane aloft until the gas ran out. Kites were the rage at that time. The object was to get the kite as high as possible using as much string as possible. When the string broke, the race was on to recover the kite, which usually wound up several blocks away.

At the beginning of summer break, we headed to our house at Lake Nuangola fifteen miles south of Wilkes-Barre. The house there was built in 1935, the same year I was born. We had electricity, indoor plumbing, a central heating system, and a well with an electric pump. Granddad's cabin was one hundred yards away and had no electricity, no central heat other than a fireplace, no running water (a hand pump outside supplied the water), and an outhouse. I never thought about it that much back then, but the outhouse was only forty feet away from the well. I will never forget the smell of the outhouse. Most of the time, I just peed in the bushes. I was always fascinated by the icebox in the kitchen. It had a peculiar odor. A local farmer, Mr. Daubert, using his horse-drawn wagon, supplied ice on Monday, meat on Tuesday, vegetables on Wednesday, and fruit on Thursday. On Friday, he would use the same wagon to pick up the garbage. I never gave much thought about that, but nobody got sick or died. On Saturday, he built stone walls, most of which survive to this day. I had fun swimming, fishing, sailing, sailboat racing (I took first place six years in a row), hiking, and building tree houses. One-half mile away was a candy store at Rule's Garage that kept me stocked with candy. The other side of the lake could be reached by way of a narrow boardwalk and bridge that crossed the swamp. Perry Storm's grocery store and an ice cream parlor were over there. It was a great hangout. One Sunday, I was sitting on the steps of the ice cream parlor when a meteorite zipped down at a low angle and hit the road not ten feet in front of me. It appeared to be about the size of a quarter and threw off sparks like a fireworks pinwheel. It made a buzzing sound and was going so fast it must have gone back into outer space.

There was also a pavilion on that side where all social gatherings were held

In 1945, Granddad gave the business to Dad and we moved to West River Street in an upscale part of the city. The house was built in 1846 and had twenty-four rooms. It still had gas lamps throughout. A front and back staircase gave my brothers and me the opportunity to chase each other throughout the house, wrecking my mother's nerves in the process. A big yard gave me plenty of space to fly smaller model airplanes. There were some neat features to the house. You could lie with your ear against the cellar floor and hear the blasting in the mines below. Our house and the house next door were on a huge rock that rolled slightly with the settling of the mines below. One year, you could put a marble at the back door and it would roll out the front door; the following year, you could put a marble at the front door and it would roll out the back door. There was never any apparent structural damage as the rolling was very slight.

I met a local boy, Dick Banta (W3TBT), who was a radio amateur. As a result, I, too, became a radio amateur (W3VCG), which led me to what I am today. I still hold those call letters. It is interesting to note that the radio amateurs  who taught me Morse code and radio theory were using spark transmitters. My travels took me from the era of spark transmitters to vacuum tubes and, eventually, transistors.

Naturally, I was attending school all of my early years. Admittedly, I did not do well in school because of what I now know to be attention-deficit disorder (ADD). It tended to make me somewhat of a loner, living in my own world of model airplanes and amateur radio. I did, however, have several neighborhood friends. Pete McCormick, down the street, and Jimmy Karambelas, across the street, became the closest. Pete went on to become a biggie in the Jesuit Church and Jimmy became a multilingual simultaneous interpreter for the United Nations. One of our many projects included unwinding a transformer and running the wire through cracks in the street to each other's houses so we could then keep in touch by Morse code.

At one point, we tried overhead wires but the bus kept knocking them down. My first transmitter was a single 6L6 amplifier tube powered by a 5U4 rectifier tube, straight out of the ARRL 1945 radio amateur's handbook. The receiver was a National Radio SW-35. The next transmitter was a Harvey Wells Bandmaster and the receiver a used Hammarlund Super Pro, both shown in the picture above. I damn near electrocuted myself one day when I reached behind it and hit a high voltage terminal. That setup, along with a better antenna, plus a general class license, allowed me to reach stations in foreign countries. I'll never forget my first foreign contact with a VE5 Canadian station.

Eventually, I began work on a 500-watt transmitter that later became a 1,000-watt unit all housed in a six-foot tall relay rack. Dad found a used National NC183D receiver that helped greatly in making hundreds of local and foreign contacts. I've kept it for memories and it still works.

CHAPTER ONE

My middle school days were spent at Meyer's High School in Wilkes-Barre. I then moved on to Wyoming Seminary prep school in Kingston, Pennsylvania. The spring following my junior year, my church put together a youth caravan (unknowingly all paid for by my father) to travel throughout Europe. There were thirteen of us. We left the port of New York aboard the steamship *Anna Salen* heading for Southampton, England. After spending a couple of days there, we moved on to the port at Le Havre, France, and from there by train to Paris. I wound up staying in a 175-year-old monastery at 46 rue de Beauregard. Our first jaunt was to Notre Dame Cathedral. Over the next several days, we visited the Louvre, Heart Catholic Church, and the Eiffel Tower. I was very impressed with the canal system and the boats moving silently up and down it.

We then moved on to Belgium, biked throughout that country, and took our bikes with us by train to Germany. Köln, Germany, was our next stop. We visited the Krupp Museum and then rode down the Ruhr River. We stopped at Essen and visited several refugee camps. Each night was spent at a youth hostel where we could get dinner, a bed, and breakfast for just twenty pfennigs (about six cents). A train took us to Dassel, and we then biked to Göttingen, Kassel, Pantenburg, Rothenberg, Herzfeld, Frankfurt, Darmstadt, Heppenheim, Heidelberg, Worms, Koblenz, Bonn, Kassel,

1

Groen, and Hanover. My leg muscles looked like Arnold Schwarzenegger's.

We took a night flight from Hanover to Berlin. The cities of the Western sector were brightly lit, but as soon as we reached the Eastern sector, it became pitch black for tens upon tens of miles. In all that blackness, I saw only one set of headlights. We landed in the Western sector of Berlin late at night and bedded down quickly. After breakfast the next morning, we took a subway to the Eastern sector. The car was blacked out. About halfway through the tunnel, the train suddenly stopped and the lights came on. Everybody except me jumped up and faced the wall. The man next to me grabbed my arm and slammed me face-first against the wall. As I looked under my arm, I could see soldiers with machine guns passing behind me. Interesting. A short while later, the lights again went out and we continued our journey. I emerged from the subway into Communist East Berlin. The people seemed to be going about their business, but there were armed Russian soldiers everywhere.

Since I had been instructed not to take a camera, I had to commit it all to memory. On one side of the boulevard was a block of high-rise buildings. Immediately, I noticed that no one was going into or coming out of those buildings. I slowly sauntered down a side street and saw the huge facade was being held up by giant wooden and steel girders. Obviously, the whole thing was for show. Once we returned to West Germany, we took ferries to Norway, Denmark, and Sweden. We spent three or four days in each of those countries. From there, the steamship *Holland Canada* took us to Portsmouth, England, and a train from there took us to London.

A member of the group and I lodged with Mr. and Mrs. Clark, who lived at 49 Dartmouth Park Hill, one of the two hills in London. The other is Parliament Hill. Then it was a bike marathon to see as many sights as possible. We saw Saint Paul's Cathedral, Saint Martin-in-the-Fields,

Westminster Bridge, the Tower of London, Tower Bridge, Trafalgar Square, Chelsea Hospital, the Thames, Exhibition Road, Lord Albert's Hall and monument, Kensington Palace, Bayswater Road, the Marble Arch, the Roosevelt statue, Grosvenor Square, Saint John's Wood, the zoo, Langhorne Palace, Parliament Square, Lambeth Palace, Piccadilly Circus, Downing Street, the Houses of Parliament, Big Ben, Westminster Church and Abbey, and Scotland Yard. That whole project took several days to complete. One day, Mr. Clark took me up to his widow's walk to see the surroundings. It was astonishing. All of the houses for miles around were one-story bungalows. The entire area had been leveled by V-1 and V-2 bombs.

It is amazing that out of all that destruction, Mr. Clarke's house survived without a scratch. At the end of that whirlwind trip, it was back to Southampton to take the steamship *Stockholm* to New York. The *Stockholm* was the same ship that later rammed and sank the *Andrea Doria*, the pride of the Italian cruise ship fleet. Glad it was later rather than sooner.

On my return, it was back to Wyoming Seminary for my senior year. It was just as hard for me as when I left for Europe (damn ADD). I wound up staying a year longer to repeat a subject I had not done well with. It was mandatory that each student had to do an oration in order to graduate. I had a fear of speaking before a large audience but finally did do it. My speech was on satellites and space stations. The information I built my oration on came from comic books, scientific publications like *Popular Science*, and my own fantasies. Considering the year was 1954, it was really far reaching, and many of the space stations that exist today are exactly as I described them.

CHAPTER TWO

After graduation, I tried Lafayette College for a year, and that was a total disaster. You don't get near any electronic engineering until your junior year, and I simply couldn't wait. Then came Rider College (now Rider University) in Trenton (Lawrenceville), New Jersey. After a couple of years at Rider, I wound up with a pregnant wife and soon a baby daughter. I felt I'd better get a job, and quickly! I hired the job placement company Snelling and Snelling, and within a few weeks they found me a job at RCA Laboratories in Princeton (Penn's Neck), New Jersey. I was hired in late 1957 as a research technician in Lab 3, the imaging devices section and research think tank.

A group of twelve established scientists were my "bosses." They included Dr. George Morton, coinventor of television as we know it today. Another was Dr. John Rudy, inventor of many image-conversion devices. One of his image intensifiers took the first pictures of the bottom of the polar ice cap and one took the picture of a single photon (one particle of light). We did that experiment by placing a cube of cesium iodide in front of an image intensifier. We waited for a gamma ray to pass through it and kick out one photon. We even took a picture of it. Others included Dr. Stan Forge, coinventor of the vidicon and other TV conversion tubes; Dr. Alfred Sommers, inventor of the iconoscope, the first image-conversion tube that made real-time video possible; Dr. Dave Kleitman, electrical/chemical engineer; Dr. Charles

Ching, inventor of many helical microwave amplifier tubes; Dr. Vladimir Nergard, one of the people instrumental in developing the Klystron tube that made radar, as we know it today, possible; Dr. Richard Klensch, who did basic engineering on a variety of projects; and many other truly brilliant minds. My job was to be their "hands." I designed and built much of the circuitry and many of the vacuum tubes (yes, I actually made the tubes in our glass shop) that permitted these men to continue with serious development.

We had unlimited use of vacuum chambers, glass working equipment, and machine shops. Guided by Dr. Kleitman, I evaporated virtually every combination of chemicals imaginable. We settled on cesium iodide doped with a bit of thallium as the most efficient evaporated phosphor. That was no small effort. It fluoresced a beautiful bright blue glow. A vacuum chamber had to be loaded with the chemical of interest and a vacuum pulled (which took roughly three-quarters of an hour). The chemical evaporated and was tested, using an electron gun, for efficiency. Then the vacuum was removed, the data noted, and the process started again. Sometimes, it took weeks to obtain satisfactory results. While working with these chemicals, I conceived a new way to perform image conversion. I noted that when a chemical evaporated, it did so at a nonlinear rate, and I saw promise in that effect. I wrote it up (see "Video Pickup Arrangement" below) and handed it to Dr. Morton, who passed it up the line. It came back with a note that it had no commercial value. However, to be on the safe side, they would issue a public technical note to destroy its patent value. I received a "thanks" of seventy-five dollars.

RCA Technical Note 476, September 1961
Video Pickup Arrangement
Martin L. Kaiser III

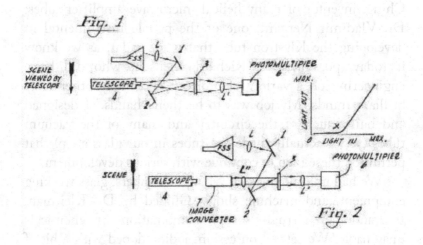

Fig. 1

Fig. 2

A video pickup of high-resolution capabilities is disclosed for picking up light rays from a remote telescope.

The arrangement shown in figure 1 includes a flying spot scanner (FSS), the concentrated light output from which is focused by means of lens L and angularly disposed mirrors 1 and 2 upon a view plate 3. The light produced in the view plate 3 is focused by lens L' upon a photo multiplier 6. This photo multiplier is provided with dynodes having secondary emission material.

View plate 3 may be a ground-glass plate with a suitable phosphor on it or a light transparent layer that supports the phosphor. The phosphor has a nonlinear characteristic as shown in figure 2. By way of example, the glass plate may be an eighth of an inch thick ground on one side and on which side the phosphor is deposited. Light from the telescope 4 is focused on the ground side of the plate.

In operation, the flying spot scanner produces a raster on the view plate. The telescope image is also placed on the view plate. The image intensity of the telescope is set below or near the threshold point X on the curve of figure 2 where the phosphor will fluoresce. The raster from the flying spot scanner is adjusted to a similar or very slightly higher level. Thus, the sum total of the light rays from both the telescope and the flying spot scanner will cause the view plate 3 to produce a light signal to which the photo multiplier 6 responds. This light signal corresponds to point-to-point scanning. The output of the photo multiplier may then be amplified to any desired level.

Figure 3 shows an arrangement for picking up a scene in the UV (ultraviolet) range. The arrangement is similar to that of figure 1, except that the image converter 7 is positioned between the output of the telescope 4 and the lens L", and the view plate is provided with a UV sensitive nonlinear phosphor. That side of the converter 7 which faces the lens L" is coated with a UV emitting phosphor. The outputs of the image converter and the flying spot scanner are in the UV portion of the frequency spectrum.

In our group, I remember four other technicians, each with his own expertise. We worked well together as a team. Although I was always sticking my nose (comments) into many, many projects other than mine, it gave me the opportunity to be part of some incredibly interesting projects, the end results of which became technology and products we take for granted today. I wrote extensively for technical journals, RCA in-house technical publications, and radio amateur magazines.

Here are some of the more interesting pieces of electronic equipment I designed and wrote about for technical and ham radio magazines. I'll do my best to explain how these devices worked.

This is a hybrid cathode modulator that used both a tube and transistors. Many radio amateurs only had continuous wave (CW) transmitters to transmit Morse code. To change those transmitters to amplitude modulated (AM) voice transmitters, they would normally need AM modulators and make extensive wiring changes to their transmitters. The hybrid modulator was an easy solution to that problem. It simply plugged into the telegraph key jack to create the AM signal.

The following is the schematic of the hybrid modulator.

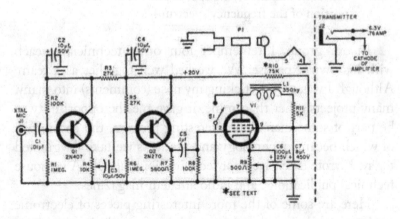

RCA developed a new, small (three-eighths inch diameter by one-half inch high) vacuum tube that they hoped would compete with the transistor. It was called the Nuvistor. The Nuvistor offered many advantages over standard size tubes but it still had a filament, the main consumer of power. Transistors have no filaments. The most important feature was that it had an extremely low noise figure (the background hiss heard when a radio is not tuned to a station) thereby permitting it to be used at very high frequencies. I saw the potential for using it in a 432 MHz (megahertz) converter. The one I built was featured in the *QST*, a publication aimed exclusively at radio amateurs. With it, I broke the distance record for that frequency. Transistors have long since surpassed the performance of my receiver.

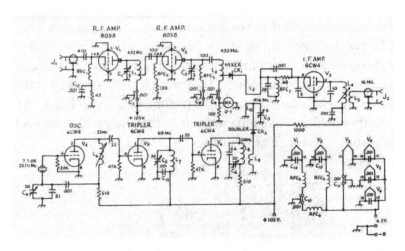

Amateur TV was a wish of many radio amateurs, but the cost of creating a picture on a distant TV set was exorbitant. An inexpensive way to get a picture on the airways was with a flying spot scanner (FSS). Based on my experience with RCA, I had good idea on exactly how to make one. The FSS is a device that

scans the screen of a picture tube, creating what is known as a raster (a blank but lighted screen). The raster consists of 525 lines scanning across the face of the tube from upper left to lower right. If no video data is applied to the electron beam, it becomes an FSS. The blank lighted screen is then focused on a photo multiplier, shown on the left side of the picture. The signal is amplified and applied to a video transmitter. To send a picture, one had only to write a message on the face of the picture tube with a black wax pencil or hold a photograph in front of the screen. This adds up to getting a picture on the airways for around $40.00.

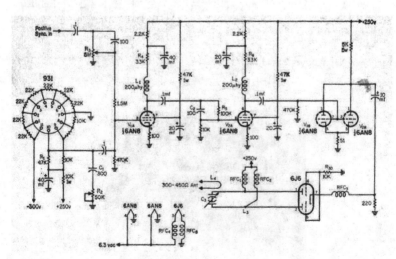

Available on the market was a World War II military camera that could be purchased for around $10.00. It used an iconoscope (the tube developed by one of my bosses, Dr. Alfred Sommers) image pickup tube. Finding one of those tubes that worked was nearly impossible. I designed a circuit for it using a more readily available pickup tube known as a vidicon (developed by Dr. Stan Forge). My modifications to the camera made getting on the airways with TV an inexpensive proposition. The picture shows what the unit looked like. The following story about this camera appeared in a collection of RCA memos.

TECHNICAL PAPERS ON AIRBORNE TELEVISION

THIS ISSUE OF RCA REVIEW contains the first of a series of technical articles on airborne television a system of sight transmission having momentous military and civilian applications. Prepared and written by scientists and engineers of Radio Corporation of America, they are presented to readers of RCA REVIEW as an historic record of pioneering and scientific progress.

The idea behind airborne television and its development originated in RCA more than twelve years ago. It was in the spring of 1934 that Dr. V.K. Zworykin formulated plans and submitted to me (David Sarnoff, president of RCA) a memorandum suggesting the creation of such a system to serve as "electronic eyes" in guiding radio-controlled aerial torpedoes. At that early date, Dr. Zworykin foresaw the threat of Japan's "Kamikaze" or Suicide Corps, and sought to achieve by technological means what the Japanese hoped to attain by psychological training was so impressed that, accompanied by Dr. Zworykin, I went to Washington and presented his plans to the War and Navy Departments. Some time elapsed before the armed services became actively interested in airborne television, but our scientists, meanwhile, continued to experiment and pioneer with this revolutionary method of extending human sight. First Ray D. Kell and Waldemar Poch developed light-weight cameras and associated equipment. Then Henry Kozanouski joined in and produced research equipment which was field tested in an airplane.

When the war emergency arrived, the entire organization was ready to meet the challenge. Three airborne television systems—designated "Block," "Ring" and "Mimo" projects as security pseudonyms—evolved for secret wartime purposes. Television pick-up and transmitting equipment that once might have filled a large room was redesigned, modified and built to "suitcase" compactness for military uses in the Block system, which was employed effectively in the war by both the Army and Navy. The heavier, long-range Ring system was developed during the final stages of the conflict by engineers of the National Broadcasting Company, Inc., in conjunction with the U.S. Navy. The Mimo equipment was the midget of the three systems, being even smaller than the Block. One of these glide

12

bombs knocked out the Japanese radar at Reboul effectively blinding the Japanese fleet.

It is understandable that I would turn my amateur radio interests toward amateur television and have my own ham TV station on the air. The picture shows me with my home-built camera and TV transmitter. At the left side of the picture is my 1,000-watt multiband AM transmitter that I started building at age fourteen. Another amateur television enthusiast, William (Bill) Haldane, and I became close friends. He was part of RCA Service Company, a group that put our ideas into the field for further trials. At that time, Dr. Klensch and others, including me, were developing several schemes involving VVLF (very, very, low-frequency) technology, below 10Hz (hertz). We used to call them "cycles" back then. One of my favorite puns was that it's easy to ride a motorcycle but try riding a motorhertz.

While waiting for the vacuum chambers to reach the desired pressure, I spent an enormous amount of time in the library scouring over Russian and German scientific papers. Although I do not read or speak either language, show me a schematic and I'll tell you what the words most likely said. One interesting item I uncovered was the Germans' use of strobe lights in an attempt to down our aircraft. They would point the strobe spotlight at our aircraft and adjust the speed of the flash so it created confusion and disorientation. On the ground, the German equipment operators were either losing consciousness or throwing up. They soon realized that one of the frequencies they had chosen, close to 6.8Hz, was the resonant frequency of the human body and the infrared component of the light caused the problem. The Germans solved the problem by wearing filter glasses that blocked the infrared component.

At the lab, we stumbled across that problem too. Tens of kilowatts of audio were generated close to the 6.8Hz frequency. As a result, lab personnel were walking into walls, tripping over chairs, and becoming disoriented.

The decision was made to stay well away from that critical frequency and conduct research elsewhere in the spectrum. We were working at those frequencies to develop a submarine communication system. In essence, we vibrated the entire earth so the deeper the submarine dove, the stronger the signal was. One of our systems was on the submarine *Thresher*, which imploded and sank.

Since we were all pretty much playing it "by ear," we had more fun than anyone should have in one lifetime. Here is a good example. Several hundred yards behind the main building was a small pond. A bridge crossed the pond and in the middle of the bridge was a small house for test equipment. A hydrophone was lowered from the house into the pond.

Two hundred yards away, a ten-foot-long by four-inch diameter rod was driven flush with the ground. Next to it lay a small loudspeaker and microphone connected to the pond house. My job was to drop a ten-pound cannonball onto the stake when Klensch yelled, "Go." He, in turn, would measure the shockwave. There I was in the middle of a field, repeatedly dropping a cannonball on the ground. Someone inside the main building noticed me and called authorities. Soon an ambulance was fast approaching across the field. My explanation caused all concerned sidesplitting laughter. After the ambulance left, Klensch and I continued with the cannonball dropping experiment.

Somehow, I stumbled upon a gold mine. As various labs would clean house, the older equipment would be sent to the basement of Lab 1 and auctioned off. Possessing this equipment would help me understand the thought process that went into just about every piece of electronic equipment the lab developed. If I wanted something, I would bid five cents. If I really wanted something, I would bid ten cents. If I really, really wanted something,

I would bid twenty-five cents. I got them all! Filled with excitement, I would take the newfound prize home to examine and show it to my wife. Her comment was usually the same: "Trash day is on Tuesday."

CHAPTER THREE

One day Bill Haldane, a fellow radio amateur, approached me and asked if I'd like to go to Trinidad. Neither he nor I knew where that was but it sounded interesting. When I got home, I grabbed the encyclopedia and found out it is in the Caribbean. After discussing it with my wife, I returned with a firm "yes." A month or two later, Bill again approached me and advised that Trinidad would not accept our presence and wondered if I would like to go to Antigua. I didn't know where that was either, but again said "yes." A month or two later, he told me that Antigua wouldn't accept our presence either. He mentioned RCA had decided to set up the project on Barbados, British West Indies, where there was a small US Navy base. They simply would not tell the Barbadian government about the project. He asked if I would go there and I responded in the affirmative, even thought I had no idea what the "project" was all about.

Finally, I was given a briefing about a new high frequency (1 to 30 MHz) "over the horizon radar" (OHR) an RCA technician/ham had conceived. Essentially, it was to study the "flutter effect" caused by objects moving through the ionosphere. In those days, thanks to the early design of limiter stages in the receiver, one could readily hear the effect when an airplane flew between an FM transmitter and FM receiver or see the effect when an airplane flew between a TV transmitter and a TV receiver. My job was to see if any useful information could be extracted from the flutter. I later learned that the two islands had turned us down because it was in the middle of the Cuban Missile Crisis and they did not want to antagonize their friend Cuba.

I was transferred to RCA Service Company and sent to Burlington, Massachusetts to check out the hardware. When I arrived in Burlington, to my astonishment, absolutely *nothing* relating to the project was there. Within three months, two technicians and I appropriated or stole (allocated but not yet delivered—midnight raids, you know) and assembled all of the equipment needed into two forty-foot trailers. Finally, the four antennas were ready to ship by air and trailers ready to be put on ships headed toward Barbados and Jamaica. My wife and I closed up the house and, along with our three- and five-year-old children, flew on probably one of the first 707s to take to the air to Barbados.

RCA would only pay for the least expensive lodging on the island and the Powell Springs Hotel met their criteria at US$25.00 per night (it is now US$2,000.00 per night). Brian Lakes, the owner of the Powell Spring, picked us up at the airport and drove us to the hotel, which was on the east coast of the island. The setting was a picture postcard: beautiful, blue Caribbean Sea with huge breakers crashing on the shore and rocks, palm trees waving in the wind and dripping of sea spray. The room was spartan, neat and clean. The fare was typically British. We spent several days there while planning for permanent lodging. I ordered a car from Johnston's Stable and Garage and a 1956 VW Beetle was delivered. To get the feel of driving on the left, we drove around the east coast for a while. We were then ready for our big trip across the island. Driving across the island was a bit of a challenge because we had arrived in the middle of the sugar cane season. Fifteen-foot-high stalks of sugar cane blocked the view from every direction and there were *no* road signs. I had to use the "spit, splat, go" form of direction finding my father taught me. That is where you spit in

17

one hand, slap your hands together, and then go in the direction of the maximum spit. It got us to the west coast.

When we reached the intersection of our cross-island road and highway 1A, a man was hammering a for rent sign into his lawn. I stopped him and asked to see the property. It was known as Highbury House and it was absolutely perfect. It had a large living/dining area that measured twenty feet wide by forty feet long, two bedrooms, and a kitchen. He said the rent was BDOS$150.00 per month and I accepted. That meant it was only US$75.00 per month. Since my daily RCA budget for lodging was US$100.00, I could pocket US$25.00. We were only one hundred feet away from the best beach on the island of Barbados: the Sandy Lane Beach. The beach is a mile long and I have many, many pictures of my family there with absolutely no other people on the beach. The water was so clear you could stand waist deep in it, look down at your feet, and see them as if you were standing in air. The kids spent their time swimming, chasing and trapping coconut crabs, roaring around the living room on their tricycles, and a million other things that kids do.

From a kid's perspective, it was like living in the world's biggest sandbox.

As soon as we were settled, I went to the navy base to announce my presence. The captain of the base reacted with total surprise. *No one* had informed him of our intention to set up on "his" base on the north coast. It turned out that the four RCA advance men never left Bridgetown (south coast), the capital city of Barbados, but instead spent their time enjoying the wonderful

Barbadian rum and the strikingly beautiful women. I was truly on my own. After some serious negotiating (and I do mean serious), the captain gave me a few hundred square feet of space on which to set up my project.

In a few weeks, the antennas arrived aboard the same 707 I had arrived on. These consisted of four fifty-foot-plus tower sections and hundreds of pounds of rope, cable, hardware, and antenna parts. In the absence of a forklift truck, it took the pilot, copilot, flight engineer, all the stewardesses, all the ground crew people I could gather, and me to get the pieces out of the airplane. Naturally, rum and beer flowed freely. They were then loaded on flatbed trucks and taken to my little piece of "land." My antenna site was to be on the beach 120 feet below, but there was a major problem waiting. Hundreds of manchineel trees (a highly poisonous tropical tree that bears a very poisonous apple) covered the beach. One drop of the sap from either the tree or apple raises a blister on the skin within seconds.

My son picked up one of the apples and threw it. He then rubbed his eye and wound up with a completely swollen and closed eye that oozed green glop for a month. After the manchineel trees were bulldozed off the beach, I began installing four (two sets of two) *huge* log periodic antennas. Two were  150-foot-long 1 to 30 MHz vertical log periodic curtains. Two were huge, and very heavy, 3 to 30 MHz horizontal log periodic beams mounted on the 100-foot towers that supported the curtain. They were to be held up by half-inch nylon rope. Working with that rope was a real exercise. When stretched, it nearly doubles in length. I hired four local

Barbadians at BDOS $1.75 (US$0.88) per day (fixed by the government) to help erect the antennas. Nearly every night, Barbadian fishermen would "liberate" some of my beautiful rope. To solve that problem, I made several meaningless medallions that my workmen had to hang around their necks while working at the antenna site otherwise they would become impotent. When word got out about that, the thefts stopped immediately.

My family and I settled into the wonderful Barbadian life, but the peace didn't last long. One day while working on the antennas, I heard the drone of a four-engine airplane and looked up to see a Russian bomber at about 1,000 feet with its bomb bay doors wide open and a very large camera sticking out. Others obviously saw the plane too, because it wasn't long before the American ambassador was banging on my door. Since my wife is the politician of the two of us, I let her handle the incident. Sure enough, after a few of her special cherry cheesecake pies, we were back on track. Those pies seemed to be the magical answer to the many other situations that would arise.

The trailer finally arrived by an interisland steamer (shades of the *African Queen*) and, you guessed it, there was no tractor on the island with which to pull it. I must have looked like Buster Keaton getting the container off the ship. When they raised the container a few feet, it began to swing from side to side and one of those sides was the Caribbean ocean! Finally, on one long swing, the captain ordered the crane brakes released and, with a loud *bang*, the container was now solidly on Barbadian soil. Several trips to the junkyard solved the tractor problem. The one I found also had no brake release compressor, so I constructed a small gasoline powered compressor to do just that. The trailer was then towed, without brakes, over mountainous terrain to my site at the navy base. My caravan consisted of myself in my 1956 VW waving a very large red flag out of the window followed by the tractor/trailer. As I passed through several small villages, many Barbadians ran out to the street, clapping their hands and jumping wildly in joy, thinking the island had been or was going to be taken over by Communists.

The Russians tried the OHR system for a while and theirs became affectionately known as the "woodpecker" to us radio amateurs because of the sound it made as it swept across the radio bands. A few years ago, my copy of *Microwave* magazine arrived and, lo and behold, my system is *still* in operation. Another version of the system was revealed in a 2002 issue of *Popular Science* that used the cell telephone and GPS systems for detection of stealth and other aircraft. The Russian OHR system was put out of business by the explosion of the atomic energy plant at Chernobyl. Radioactive dust literally covered the OHR site. That was a real shame because the Russians beat us hands down with their system.

My project ended in the midst of a major political disaster. There were far too many stateside managers arguing amongst themselves that they lost sight of what the project was all about. I was happy to get off the island and it actually worked out well with my family. Stateside, it was the start of the school year.

Here is a cartoon my friends
at RCA gave me.

CHAPTER FOUR

On my return to the United States, the RCA Service Company at Cherry Hill, New Jersey didn't know exactly what to do with me. I had been a bad boy for suggesting that Raytheon be given the follow-up contract. My boss put me to work in the basement of his house (obviously to hide me) building a frequency standard for the Nimbus satellite. I approached RCA Labs in Princeton about changing my title from Senior Technician to Associate Engineer because I had, under very difficult conditions and circumstances, acted as international diplomat and single handedly managed, designed, built, refined, and operated a major multi-million dollar project. They  essentially said that since I did not have an engineering degree, I was a "certifiable dummy."

That was the end of my career with RCA. For a brief period, I worked at Telerad Manufacturing in Flemington, New Jersey, a division of the Lionel Corporation (maker of toy trains). There, I developed and oversaw the manufacturing of, among other products, the command receiver for the Atlas missile. The picture to the right shows me with my left hand on the command receiver mounted on the shake table. A shake table is used to determine if the receiver could withstand the rigors of a rocket flight. The large item at the lower left of the picture is the driver for the shake table. Next to my right hand is the indicator test panel for the receiver. To the left of my left hand are the two power supplies for the receiver and indicator panel. On top of the power supplies is the channel simulator and to the right of that is the signal generator that drives the shake table. I made the test panel and channel simulator. All receivers passed all tests.

On a humorous note, I was sent to corporate headquarters in New Brunswick, New Jersey to review a bid on another product. I declined the bid. While I was there, they were testing aluminized toy balloons to see if they could hold the helium under high temperature. An entire room was filled with the balloons and the heat turned to maximum. They forgot to tell the janitor about the balloon test, so when he entered the room and found the heat stifling, he opened all the windows and a huge mass of aluminized balloons exited the room. Radars at the three New York airports saw the unidentified blip and thought it was a UFO.

Petrovend Corporation asked Telerad (me) to develop a dollar bill changer. It used the transparency of the bill as the key benchmark in accepting it. They wanted to put the changer into all of their gas pumps. Eventually they dropped the project when credit cards made the scene.

I returned to college to receive my degree in business administration. Most likely with RCA's comment in mind along with being more mature, I totally surprised my wife and myself by spending all remaining semesters on the dean's list. While at college, I took up flying. I put in hundreds of enjoyable hours in a Piper J3. Upon graduation, I looked for a job in the field of avionics. Narco Aviation Company hired me to work at their marine facility in Cockeysville, Maryland. The company, Enac Triton, made LORAN receivers (they are used to pinpoint your location while at sea) and was essentially a one-man show. Our type A personalities did not blend well. After three months, it was obvious that I couldn't work for him. We got into a "You can't fire me; I *quit*" argument, and that was the end of my employment. Actually, being fired was the *best* thing that ever happened to me. To keep food on the table, I took a writing job with Aircraft Armaments Incorporated (AAI). I left a few weeks later after getting into an argument with my boss over the use of a colon versus a semicolon. Really.

I had met Hallie Rice, the owner of meter manufacturer Edgerly Instrument Labs (EIL), at Enac Triton. He asked if I could help him out of a bind. He had built fifty meters for the US Navy and they were rejected by the government inspector. I had to remove all of the internal wiring and completely rewire the meters. They were then accepted. I had just made my first "real money" as an independent businessman. Hallie sold his company to Unitec Industries. Based on my relationship with him, they asked me to join their staff. Unitec purchased a small California-based company, Tracer Systems, manufacturer of bugging (eavesdropping) equipment. That company became my responsibility. Unitec also bought Police Systems, another California-based manufacturer of bugging equipment. Police Systems was owned by Bob Jefferies. Bob also had a contract with Disney to purchase, train, and care for the theatrical birds used by Disney. I had dinner with Bob one night and a parrot was on its perch at the end of the table. Once we were all seated, the parrot asked, "Is John there?"

Bob said, "No."

The parrot then asked, "Is Lila there?"

Bob said "No."

The parrot asked if Jenny was there and Bob said, "No." By then, the parrot knew my name so it asked if Marty was there.

Bob said "No."

Then the parrot asked if Bob was there and Bob said, "No." With that, the parrot laughed hysterically as it climbed up and down its perch.

Bob's electronic company was also was put under my wings. I produced a whole line of wide-band FM (WBFM) and narrow-band FM (NBFM) self-excited and crystal-controlled bugging devices and receivers—a portent of things to come.

One day in 1964, I came home, put my fist through the plasterboard wall, and announced to my wife that I was starting my own company. I had had enough of working for someone else. Naturally, she went into a panic. Not knowing exactly how to start a company, I picked up the telephone book, looked in the Yellow Pages, and called the maintenance department of the first industry listed: Armco Steel. They agreed to give me a try and handed me an inoperative Curtis Immerscope. An immerscope is a device that ultrasonically looks through a red-hot steel ingot to find flaws or air bubbles. I took it home in the trunk of my '57 Chevy, cleaned it up, and replaced all the high-voltage wiring that had become brittle from extreme heat of the steel mill with Teflon-coated wire. The maintenance manager, Fred Vogelgesang, was ecstatic. He told me to "sit" while he called several of his equivalent maintenance managers in other companies to tell them he had finally found the man they had been looking for. Within weeks, I had over twenty industrial customers all within easy driving distance. Initially, I was uncertain about how much to charge my customers.

One day at 2:00 a.m., I received an emergency call from Fred. Their vacuum degassing furnace had been damaged by some molten steel in the wrong place. This furnace measured twenty feet in diameter and twenty feet deep and could accept a large ladle of molten steel. Its load cell system (scale) was accurate to within less than one pound at 100,000 pounds.

I climbed down inside the furnace and found the burned wiring. A few quick repairs had it up and running in no time. I billed them $200.00. A few days later, Fred called and asked me to stop by; I did. He told me that Armco would have lost roughly $20,000.00 (in 1965 dollars) were it not for my timely and prompt repairs and had the steel awaiting the degassing furnace hardened. He handed the invoice back to me and told me to add another zero. *I was on my way!* Obviously, I was wrong in charging only an hourly rate for my time when I should have been charging for the value of the service from the customer's perspective. I was also given their two-way radios to repair. After watching the workmen shout into their radios to overcome the noise of the mill, I installed high-pass audio filters in each radio that blocked out the noise of the mill. The workers were not sure what had happened but they liked my modifications.

My customers included steel mills, copper refineries, bottling companies, plastic companies, ice cream cone manufacturers, plastic and paper cup manufacturers, canning companies, veneer manufacturers, breweries, and nearly one hundred more. My '57 Chevy was a blue streak Earl Schieb Special (that was a "paint your whole car including the tires for $19.95" company—just kidding about the tires). Most of the time, I was repairing process control systems, but at Kennecott Copper, I also repaired their closed-circuit television (CCTV) system. Copper ore was brought in by ship, smelted, and cast into ingots measuring twenty-five feet long by three feet high by six inches thick. Twenty of these ingots were then placed into an electrolytic bath, each separated by a thin sheet of pure copper of the same dimension but only one-sixteenth of an inch thick. Power was applied and the raw copper was electroplated to the thin sheet, resulting in an ingot of pure copper. After the ingots were removed, the bottom of the tank was dredged. The dredge was run through a kiln to dry and placed in fifty-gallon size cardboard drums.

Enter the TV camera. All of the employees had huge afro hairdos. At the end of their shift, they would take a few handfuls of dried sludge, which contained significant amounts of gold, silver, and platinum, and sprinkle it in their hair. At home, they would shake it out, take it to a jeweler, and earn a few extra dollars. The TV camera was supposed to stop that process, but since no one bothered to watch the monitor, the practice continued. To reach the camera, I had to climb a *tall* ladder and sit on a steel beam. On returning to the floor, my pants seemed a bit drafty in back. Acid had eaten off the seat of my pants.

The copper ingots were smelted and allowed to run out of a one-inch diameter hole in the bottom of the ladle, forming a one-inch diameter rod. From there, it then went to the wire, pipe, and sheet mill. I also repaired their temperature gauges and two-way radios.

When called by my first brewery, American Brewery, I quickly learned that when the "new" beer comes down the pipes early in the morning, it was mandatory for all employees, including me, to drink as much beer as possible while the pipes and machinery cooled down. I was on a first-name basis with many famous cockroaches. In a brewery, it is impossible to get rid of those little critters even with soapy, superheated steam. I considered American the most honest brewery I visited. Their taproom was a twenty-foot square room with a table and chairs in the middle. A single spigot from which beer was poured protruded from one wall and on the opposite wall was the urinal—a beer drinker's dream! It was after one of my brewery trips I got lost in downtown Baltimore (can't imagine why). I passed a gate that said "US Army Intelligence, Fort Holabird." Hey, perhaps they too had something to fix, so I drove around the property until I found a door that said "Supplies."

CHAPTER FIVE

A simple knock on that door put me into the "intelligence business." Capt. Bob Doms, the officer who ran the equipment facility, showed me several shelves of equipment that needed repair. Those included lie detectors, recorders, transmitters, receivers, meters, amplifiers, and more. Once it became obvious that I knew what I was doing, I was invited to attend several of the classes taught at the intelligence school. Their primary tools were the FG Mason A2 countermeasure receiver, a Simpson multimeter, and a wire impedance test set. The students were building their own audio amplifiers. I proposed that I manufacture the audio amplifier for them, which would in turn open up a big block of time useful elsewhere. My offer was accepted and the 1059 audio amplifier/preamplifier was born. Don't ask me how I picked that number other than it sounded good. I would build over 10,000 of them during my fifty years in business. Don't forget, I was a one-man company with a part-time secretary. The 1059 became the basic tool used in locating wired microphones. Requests for the 1059 also flowed in from other intelligence agencies, which gave me access to virtually every federal intelligence agency in the country. The Vietnam War was starting to build in intensity, so the intelligence school began inviting state and local law enforcement agencies to attend. That opened the marketplace to an even larger number of potential customers.

Marketing my products was a snap since I could now walk into virtually every intelligence agency in the Baltimore/Washington/Virginia area without escort or security badge. I also began teaching courses on bugging and bug detection at the Fort Holabird intelligence school. That gave me access to other good marketplaces. The workload of the intelligence business got so heavy that I began to cut back on industrial repairs.

Using my technical expertise, I began to develop and manufacture a whole host of products for the intelligence community. Next on the list was a countermeasure kit that would contain every electronic tool needed to perform a countermeasure sweep. Included in it were the 1019 (a 1059 with integral power amplifier and speaker), 2050CA radio frequency (RF) detector, 2030 carrier current probe, 2040 test oscillator for use with the 2050CA and 2030, an ultraviolet light, an AM/FM radio with the automatic frequency control disabled (this allowed listing to a surveillance transmitter snuggled next to a strong FM station to avoid detection); an audio test probe; and a host of hand tools and soldering products. The eighty-five-pound kit was nicknamed the "2Hern" because it would give you a double hernia if you tried to lift it. The FBI asked if I could build a scaled-down version of the kit. As a result, the 1040 countermeasure kit made the scene. It had all of the electronic tools the 2Hern had, but instead of individual hand tools, it had a compact Excelite tool pack with all of the necessary hand tools. All of it fit in a standard American Tourister attaché case. It really looked neat. Right off the bat, I sold sixty-four of them to the FBI.

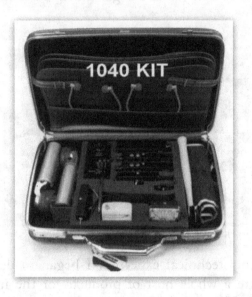

To replace the wire analyzer in use at the school, I designed and produced the battery operated 1080D telephone analyzer. It had meters and circuits to measure the telephone line voltage (to detect parallel devices), loop current (to test for series devices), hook-switch bypasses, radio frequency (RF) devices, audio on line, tone-activated devices, and virtually every other conceivable test on the telephone instrument and telephone line. The 1080D tended to overwhelm the user, so I printed a collection of three by five flash cards to show the proper switch and control position for each test. The 1080D became the standard of the intelligence community.

Requesting Office	Date of Request	Item	Quantity	Unit Cost	Receiving U.S. Department or Agency
OS	3/23/72	Telephone Analyzer	1	1,350	BNDD
TSD	5/16/72	Transmitters, Radio Beacon	8	313	BNDD
OS	3/23/72	Telephone Analyzer	1	1,350	White House Communications Agency
OS	3/23/72	Telephone Analyzers	15	1,400	Air Force
OS	3/23/72	Telephone Analyzers	10	1,350	State
OS	3/23/72	Telephone Analyzers	2	1,375	AEC
TSD	11/16/72	Camera Sets	20	656	FBI
TSD	4/17/72	Camera Sets	10	730	FBI
TSD	11/18/71	Actuators, Recorders	50	488	FBI
TSD	4/19/72	Tessina Cameras	3	730	BNDD
TSD	12/ 7/72	Camera, Video	1	18,045	FBI
TSD	10/13/72	Tube, Image, Burn-Resistance, Equivalent of W L 30691	1	4,659	FBI
TSD	3/26/71	Tubes, Image, W L 30691	2	4,007	FBI
TSD	4/20/73	Cameras, Television	2	15,320	FBI

00118

Above is a document showing some of my customers. The Air Force wanted theirs painted blue, which accounts for the slightly higher price.

As my knowledge and understanding of the electronic countermeasure business grew, I developed and manufactured a host of products. Here are just a few of them.

1009 (UAA1)/1029 miniature audio amplifiers. Unlike the 1059/1019 with their multiple input and output jacks, the 1009/1029 had only one input and one output jack.

1079 audio amplifier/speaker for use with the 1009/1029/1059 and 2050CA.

1080AVS AC-powered (110V/220V) vector oscilloscope for measuring capacitance and inductance. This product was specifically designed for telephone countermeasures but offered numerous applications.

1080CT battery-operated cable and component test set. This was a battery-operated 1080AVS and had better resolution.

1080H, a telephone analyzer similar to the 1080D but for use with electronic telephones (the type that exist today)

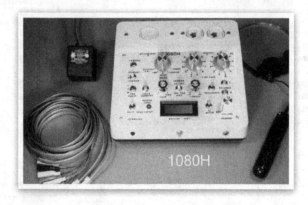

2020 acoustic noise generator to prevent interception of room conversation.

2044 desktop broadband bug detector; covered from 1 to 5,000 megahertz (MHz).

2045A: a bug detector using the "feedback" detection method. That is where the 2045A hears the bug and the bug hears the detector, which sets up a feedback squeal. It is designed for those with a weak technical background.

2046I tape recorder detector. It detected the bias oscillator used to pre-erase the tape before recording on it. Recorders no longer use bias oscillators.

2052 wired microphone detector; used a "comb" RF generator to illuminate wires and detect a wired microphone.

2055HA nearfield RF detector; for use in an area saturated with high-powered radio stations.

2057A automatic scanning receiver.

2060/2062 wearable bug and tape recorder detectors.

2065 under desktop bug detector.

4059H/4059LM/4059U/4059LH/4059C non-linear junction detectors for locating transmitters and microphones, 6080A modified Cushman CM-15 wide band spectrum analyzer shown with 1079 speaker. I later switched to an AVCOM spectrum analyzer, which I also modified.

7059/7059Q/7059QR tunable low-pass and high-pass filters to tune out unwanted noises.

8080 ultraviolet lamp for detecting fingerprints.

AUT9/SLR9 silent line tracer for tracing telephone lines, power lines, and any other line pairs while they are in use.

IR59 infrared bug detector.

PB-10 pipe banger; vibrated pipes, air conditioning ducts, and walls to prevent use of a contact microphone to pick up room conversation.

RA10/RA15 Piezo electric telephone ringer; replaced the telephone ringer that can be used to monitor room conversation while the telephone is hung up.

RAS515. The picture below shows the total array of equipment needed to create a picture. Upper left is an Avcom PSA-65 spectrum showing a video signal on the screen. Below left is an SCD-5 carrier current detector. To the right of the SCD-5 is a switching matrix that controls the route of the analyzer video and carrier-current demodulator. Center is the VM-515 video demodulator. On top of the oscilloscope is the RAS515 that controls the height, width, and intensity of the output signal. The oscilloscope displays the resulting picture.

SCD-5/SCD-50/SCD-500 low-frequency (5 KHz to 700 KHz) carrier-current receivers; detected transmitters on the telephone lines, cable TV, AC power lines, or any other wire pair.

SLC9/SLR9 ultrasonic silent wire communicators; used to covertly communicate over a telephone line while the telephone was in use.

VCD (video feedback detector). This was simply a lamp flasher. It was placed in a lamp to cause the lamp to flash on and off. If a TV transmitter was present, the change in raster buzz could be heard clearly with a 2050CA bug detector ($300.00). It effectively replaced the $200,000.00 receiver then in use by the intelligence community.

VLF59 low frequency receiver/converter; converted 10 KHz to 1 MHz up to 1 MHz to 2 MHz. Most spectrum analyzers in use at that time only covered down to 1 MHz. This unit permitted monitoring to as low as 10 KHz.

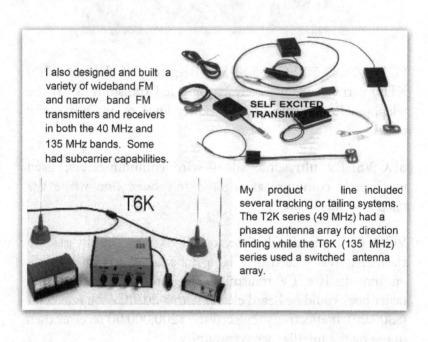

I also designed and built a variety of wideband FM and narrow band FM transmitters and receivers in both the 40 MHz and 135 MHz bands. Some had subcarrier capabilities.

SELF EXCITED TRANSMITTERS

T6K

My product line included several tracking or tailing systems. The T2K series (49 MHz) had a phased antenna array for direction finding while the T6K (135 MHz) series used a switched antenna array.

CHAPTER SIX

By the early 70s, I had close to 200 customers. They included corporations large and small and foreign, federal, state, and local governments.

When I began selling countermeasure equipment and teaching at Fort Holabird, Larry Linville, a Washington, DC police officer, approached me and asked about using my 1059 and 1059XM contact microphones for bomb work. I listened to his stories about working on suspicious packages and it became obvious that the 1059 needed an automatic gain (volume) control (AGC). I then began manufacturing the 2049BDA that met most of his requirements. Sgt. Mike Lizak of the US Army Picatinny Arsenal explosive ordnance facility bought hundreds of them. It became standard equipment for all military explosive ordnance disposal (EOD) groups.

Of all my efforts, I drew the most satisfaction from the design, development, and manufacture of bomb detection equipment. It saved lives. As this story unfolds, you will read of my thought process on how each product evolved. Wording will be selected very carefully in order not to encourage anyone to build a bomb.

To discourage that, it may interest you to know that most bomb makers blow themselves up.

In the mid-60s, most cities did not have dedicated bomb squads. Some of the larger cities, like New York and Los Angeles, had people who regularly did their bomb work but it was usually secondary to their primary functions. Larry Linvel of the Metro DC bomb squad introduced me to other police officers who were doing this "double duty." Lt. Gil Karner of the Baltimore City Police Department bomb squad and I became close friends. Gil told me about a loosely knit association of bomb technicians that was forming from Florida to California to Boston. I accepted his invitation to join the group. I am now a charter and life member of the association. It became obvious, for a variety of reasons, that we would need input from crime scene investigators, so they, too, were asked to join. The group eventually became known as the International Association of Bomb Technicians and Investigators (IABTI). The IABTI consisted of local and regional chapters operating under an international leadership. It was during the chapter and regional meetings that I developed many of my ideas for new products. We would discuss a recent bombing and methods to defeat it should it happen again. By the next meeting, I usually had a new product related to the bombing to show. It usually took me two weeks from concept to finished product.

Here are a few of them.

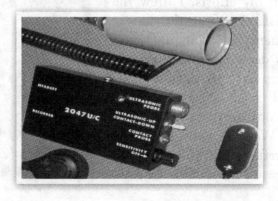

I heard the Marine barracks bombing in Beirut, Lebanon used a gas-enhanced device. Knowing escaping gas produces most of its sound in the ultrasonic region, I immediately produced the 2047U/C ultrasonic and contact/stethoscope. It became the new standard for all military bomb squads.

To counter radio-controlled devices, magnetic fields, and command detonation devices, I produced the 2079RCM. I sold only two. When I saw the shortcomings of the product, I bought both back and replaced them with a 2055H nearfield detector, a 2099 magnetic field detector, and a 2087 current detector.

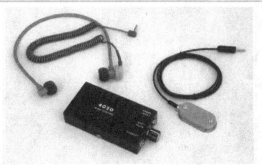

Most bomb techs were buying their equipment out of pocket. I saw the need for a scalded down version of the 2049BDA. I probably gave away as many 4020s mini-stethos as I sold.

The 2010/2010A Doppler stethoscopes were truly amazing devices. I had accidently discovered the principle behind the homodyne module (transmitter and receiver combined) while working on my Super Man X-ray which I envisioned being able to see inside packages. With them you could hear timers inside soft sided packages such as cardboard boxes, attache cases, suitcases and even PVC pipes. It also detected radio controlled improvised explosive devices.

The picture below shows me at an IABTI conference with a Safeco bomb suit. Dragging around a mannequin to put it on was a real chore. Imagine checking in a body at the airport. I took off its head, arms, and legs and taped them together. I had a carrying bag made so the body wouldn't scare the heck out of someone. In the lower right corner is a Canadian manufactured disrupter or water cannon.

The IRD59-2 detects the presence of an infrared (IR) trip-beam being used either for alarm purposes or triggering of an improvised explosive device (IED). The system consists of the detector assembly, IR probe with detectors on two sides covered with a Wratten IR filter, probe extension cable, and high impedance headset. The detector contains an integral I.R. TEST led that transmits a 1,000 hertz tone for testing the system. One nine-volt and one AA alkaline battery power the unit. The unit detects the following types of IR beams and reacts as described.

As the probe is passed through the IR beam, either the yellow *left* light emitting diode (LED) or the red *right* LED will light. When the IR source is to the left of the unit, the *left* LED flashes and an internal vibrator pulses on and off. When the IR source is to the right of the unit, the *right* LED remains lit and the vibrator runs continuously. The unit detects both continuous wave and modulated beams.

The POW-GAL 27 blasting machine (right) became the workhorse for the EOD community. It contained a charged capacitor firing circuit and a built-in test meter (galvanometer). This unit was designed for use with standard blasting caps. I sold thousands of them locally and internationally. I also made a POW-GAL 150 for use with conductive silver igniters.

I foresaw the use of radioactive material in an IED and offered the Victoreen Geiger counter (right) to counter that threat. It didn't have to be bomb-grade radioactive material but could be as simple as radioactive material from oil drilling rigs, non-destructive testing labs, or hospitals. A large firecracker could easily spread radioactive material throughout the lobby of an office building, making it uninhabitable.

Below are three different metal detectors. To the far left is a Garrett detector. It is a pulse induction all-metal detector with circuity to eliminate ground effect. It detects all metal. Below is a Schonstedt magnetometer. It only detects ferrous material. It is particularly useful in finding the blasting caps in land mines. I represented both of these companies. To the right is my model 8010G beat frequency detector. In operation, an internal oscillator is set to the same frequency as the external oscillator (probe). When the probe is brought near metal, the pitch of the output tone as heard through the headset increases. When brought near mineral material (i.e., plastic explosive), the pitch of the output tone decreases.

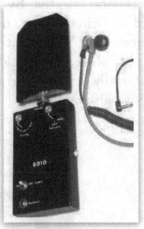

Hasting Fiberglass made several fiberglass poles and accessories that were useful to bomb technicians. I represented Hasting.

To the right is a liquid nitrogen dispersal system. In use, a dike of insulating foam is made around the IED. The dike is filled with liquid nitrogen, which freezes the battery.

Here are some of my other EOD/IED products.

4022, a stereo stethoscope. It is mainly useful in hostage situations. The two probes are placed on a structure, such as a wall, as far apart as possible. It is then possible to determine the location of an individual on the other side of the wall.

2046I, an inductive stethoscope. It is used primarily to find a digital clock timer located in an IED.

2049R/T, a transmitter and receiver used to extend the distance between a 2049BDA stethoscope and a listening post. Typical range is 1,000 feet.

4036R/T, a bomb suit communication system.

4040DLT (down line talker); it is used to communicate over the blasting line.

7079X, a multifunction stethoscope; it included an amplifier, tone filter, and speaker.

Life Sciences. I offered a chemical/biological suit, gas mask, cleaning detergent, and kiddy pool.

Buckey/MinXray. There were three X-rays used by bomb technicians. I represented Buckey and MinXray. Both of these were 70 kilovolt X-rays and were primarily useful on soft-sided packages such as letters, cardboard boxes, attachés, and suitcases. The other X-ray is a 270-kilovolt unit made by Golden Engineering. He sold direct to bomb squads. His unit could see through pipe bombs.

Rather than sitting around drinking beer and telling war stories, we decided to add some educational fun to the meetings. At chapter and regional meetings it was mandatory that each bomb technician bring his or her own "inert" bomb. Obviously, no explosives were involved. However, to indicate that the bomb technician had failed in his or her effort to disarm the "bomb," we permitted buzzers, flashbulbs, and small firecrackers with a cracked light bulb inserted to "announce" the failure. There were a *lot* of failures! I absorbed all of their ideas on disarming and some were pretty unique. Letter bombs were always a problem. Radio Shack had a contact cleaner spray that could be sprayed on an envelope. It would make the paper transparent enough to see the contents. It also worked on packages using lightweight cardboard. Several methods of handling pipe bombs were shown. Unfortunately, some of the procedures were downright dangerous. Keep in mind that the disrupter or water cannon had yet to enter the picture. Hook and line techniques were taught at Redstone Arsenal and relayed by word of mouth to other techs. I translated as many ideas as I could into detection products. Some worked great and some eventually proved to be of little or no value. My name became widely recognized throughout the bomb technician community as the source for creative equipment ideas.

It wasn't until we took our ideas out of the classroom and into the field that I experienced my first explosions. It seemed that IABTI members had an unending supply of explosives for training exercises. There also seemed to be an unending supply of cars and buildings to blow up. Usually, we would strategically place a pound or two of explosives at the "seat" of the explosion in a recent typical bombing incident. A discussion of the bombing would follow. We would then carefully look over the car to see where various objects were located inside. Then we would back off a thousand feet or so, someone would yell, "Fire in the hole!" *Kablam!* The car would fly into a jillion pieces. After we put out any fire, we returned to the car to learn every detail of the explosion. What type of explosive was it? Military or civilian? Where were the explosives placed? How many pounds? How far did the parts fly? What route did the explosion take as it ripped the car apart? Who would have died? We asked a whole bunch of other questions.

I have fond memories of one of those exercises held in Atlanta, Georgia. Explosives were placed at two locations in the car: in the trunk and on the steering column. We fired the trunk first, did a cursory examination, and then fired the one on the steering column. We then made a detailed examination of the "crime scene." After enjoying some of the always present and ice-cold beer, one of the techs pulled out a six-pound military shape charge. It was placed directly over the engine block of a car to see what damage it would do. We retreated farther than normal. After the obligatory "Fire in the hole!", the charge went off and it knocked most of us off our feet. The hood went flying about one thousand feet in the air. It crumpled into the shape of a hang glider wing and off it flew like the space shuttle coming in for a landing. We watched as it disappeared from view over the horizon. We heard nothing over the police radio, so we assumed it didn't decapitate anyone or knock a plane out of the sky. We went back to what was left of the car and there was the engine block, straight down in a hole about ten feet deep.

In another exercise, Sir Tom Brodie of the Miami, Dade County, Florida bomb squad wanted to show off his new bomb containment vehicle. It consisted of a half-inch thick steel bowl four feet in diameter with an open top, sides about three feet high, and sand in the bottom, all mounted on a trailer. We placed a few sticks of dynamite in the vessel as a test. It was an overcast day with the ceiling at about one thousand feet. When the dynamite was detonated, the shock wave flew up and bounced off the low ceiling and returned to nearly flatten us all. At the same time, there were some crows flying by and they took a rapid trip into the unknown. The shock wave blew a perfect hole through all of the cloud layers and you could see the pretty blue sky above.

The city of Virginia Beach gave us a building they no longer needed and we were free to blow it to pieces. We fired off a whole bunch of improvised bombs inside the building to see their effects. Then, we got serious. There were two identical rooms in the building. We put tables and chairs in each and taped pictures to the walls with duct tape. One-quarter pound of C4 military plastic explosive was placed on each table. One room was left as it was but the other was filled with firefighting foam to see if it could suppress the blast. We detonated the explosive in the first room and doors, windows, pieces of the table, and chairs flew everywhere. We detonated the explosive in the second room and all we heard was a loud *whoomp*. Nothing flew. Once the foam was blown out of the room by fire fighters' fans, we could see that the table had a big hole in it, but the chairs were sitting where they were and the pictures were still on the wall. Chalk one up for firefighting foam.

We had heard a great deal about military shaped charges and the wonders they could perform, but they were not readily available to the average technician. We decided to try some ideas on the building. Someone mentioned that filling a Tupperware bowl with water and wrapping the bowl with detonating cord would make an improvised shape charge. We promptly put one together and propped it against the outside wall using a two by four. The device was detonated and, sure enough, it knocked a four-foot diameter hole through the cinderblock wall.

CHAPTER SEVEN

I would eventually teach surveillance and countersurveillance not only at the Holabird School but also at the Pennsylvania State Police academy in Hershey, Pennsylvania. I taught bomb detection and disposal at the Navy EOD School in Indian Head, Maryland and Hazardous Devices School at Redstone Arsenal in Huntsville, Alabama for over twenty years.

The picture to the left shows me at one of my Pennsylvania State Police A classes. On my right side is the director of the school, Capt. James Regan. In the second row middle is Sgt. Leo Moran. To his left is Trooper Fred Rokosky and to the far right is Trooper Rocky Rockwell. The rest of the people were students from various state and federal agencies.

As my reputation spread, I would be asked to perform electronic countermeasure sweeps and lecture on electronic surveillance and counter surveillance as well as on bomb detection and disposal.

Milton Allen, the Baltimore City States Attorney, was running a drug task force and he felt they were being bugged. Once in his office, I performed a countermeasure sweep for radio frequency transmitters and wired microphones. None were found. There was a ten-pair terminal block in the main office which led to a twenty-pair terminal block in the waiting room with a cable leading to the basement. The first four pairs on the terminal blocks had telephones on them and each exhibited normal line voltage, loop current, and dial tone level—all key indicators. I decided to test for voltage on the remaining unused pairs of wires and there was none. I then tested the resistance of each pair. On the fifth pair of terminals, I found a near short. I connected my 1059 amplifier to those terminals, lifted one of the telephone handsets and could clearly hear a dial tone. I thought, *What is this? No line voltage but telephone audio?* I had just uncovered the most unique wiretap I had ever seen.

The wire tapper had used one of the unused wires from the twenty-pair terminal block that ran to the ten-pair terminal block. At the ten-pair block end, he or she attached another unused wire that ran back to the twenty-pair terminal block. From that point, the wire tapper used another unused wire that went back to the ten-pair block. The wire tapper repeated this exercise ten times and, in essence, built a ten-turn transformer inside the cable. That resulted in the ability to monitor any of the four telephones. I went to the basement and found the pair of wires that went to the transformer he or she had built. A fifty-gallon cardboard container sat near the wires. There was dust on the cover of the container that revealed where the recorder had been placed. An ashtray filled with butts was still there.

Maryland State Trooper Norval Cooper, Maryland Governor Marvin Mandel's personal bodyguard, asked me to do a sweep of the governor's office. I did a countermeasure sweep for radio frequency transmitters and microphones and found none. Before I move on to the telephone, you should know a bit of how they work. When the telephone is hung up, the two incoming wires are connected to two switches that are open circuited. Another switch across the earpiece is closed and the earpiece effectively shorted. When the telephone handset is picked up, the two switches simultaneously close and the earpiece contact opens to allow an outgoing call or answer an incoming call. The earpiece is then not only a speaker but one of the best dynamic microphones known. Think of it this way. When electricity goes in, sound comes out and when sound goes in, electricity comes out. If the switch across the earpiece is defeated, i.e., bent, and two spare wires connected across the earpiece, it is possible to monitor room conversation while the telephone is hung up. That is exactly what happened to Governor Mandel's Red Hot Line telephone. I left it to Sgt. Cooper to find the listening post and was never told its location.

The country's largest platinum refiner requested a sweep. They were primarily interested in their board room. I did the usual sweep for RF transmitters and optical devices and found none. I found no wired microphones under the conference table or carpets, inside electrical outlets and switches, behind baseboards, and many other locations. The room had a dropped ceiling, so I got a step ladder and examined the area above the ceiling. I discovered no wired microphones. There was, however, a Muzak loudspeaker in the ceiling. Knowing that loudspeakers can also be microphones, as in the Governor Mandel case, I traced the wire to a janitorial maintenance closet. When I looked behind the Muzak receiver, I found a two-position switch. When in the on position, it connected the music to the board room. In the other position, it connected the speaker to a matching transformer and tape recorder. The recorder was still in place and whoever was using it was able to record all board meetings. I got a *big* thanks for that find and a nice fat check.

Clay Shaw, one of my Holabird students, asked me to do a sweep at the Phillip Morris cigarette paper plant in High Point, North Carolina. A hostile labor strike was in progress. I did the usual sweep and found four wiretaps. It turns out they were put there by the guy who hired me. During the sweep, I found a need for an RCA connector so I went to the local Radio Shack. When I went in, there was a queue of three men, two white and one black, so I stood at the end of the line. When the black man turned around and saw me, he said, "Excuse me sir" and promptly took his place behind me. When I got to the counter, I stepped aside and said, "This gentleman (the black man) is next." With that, the manager of the store ran around the counter, grabbed me by the shirt collar and belt, and threw me out the door. The black man followed shortly afterward. It took me a while to figure out what had happened, but I got out of there quickly. I did without the connector. Oh, I forgot to mention that while I was doing the sweep, someone took a shot at me. It missed. Clay was later killed in a shootout with the Dutch (Holland) police.

I was asked to perform a counter eavesdropping sweep for the Canadian prime minister. I packed my equipment and headed to Toronto. On landing, the pilot came on the intercom and said, "Mr. Kaiser, please come to the front of the airplane." I expected a royal welcome but instead, the pilot yanked me into the cockpit and asked, "What do you have in your attaché that's beeping?" I told him that the beeper I use during sweeps must have gone off. I told him not to worry about it; I would turn it off inside the terminal. He said, "You see that attaché case out there in the middle of the tarmac? That's yours." Embarrassed, the pilot and I went out to the case, opened it, and turned the beeper off. He was amazed and interested in the contents of the kit, so I gave him a sales pitch. Hey, never pass up an opportunity. When I turned toward the airplane, I could see the passengers with their noses pressed against the window.

My trip was probably the most advertised sweep ever known. I never found anything in the prime minister's office. The sweep was in the mid-80s and I can imagine what would happen today. I did find a tracking transmitter on the car of one of the secretaries.

Puerto Rico has always been one of my favorite destinations. I never knew what humor lay around the next bend. The Puerto Rico Police bought a 1040 countermeasure kit and a 1080D telephone analyzer and asked me to do a training session at their academy. Except for the language barrier, the kit training went off without a hitch. The telephone analyzer worked fine on individual telephone instruments, but measuring the telephone line parameters was a waste of time. There was only a single conductor/wire where one would normally expect two. The second conductor was a brass plate in the outhouse. There would have to be a similar brass plate in the outhouse at the far end. The system had a line voltage ranging from six to seventy volts (the normal is forty-eight volts). It varied in proportion to the amount of rain that had fallen and the amount of crap and piss in the outhouse. They had to use the single conductor system because subversives kept cutting down the wire.

The academy was in the mountains with little else around. My host took me to a wooden shack for lunch. The walls inside were covered with eight by ten photographs of rabbits and in the middle of the room was a large bubbling pot of rabbit carcasses. I took a couple of legs, which was about as much as I could handle. That evening, I spent time with my head hanging over the toilet bowl.

While there, I also did a countermeasure sweep of the governor's office and residence and found nothing. He really did live well.

My next trip was a visit with the Puerto Rico bomb squad. They wanted me to train them on dealing with improvised explosive devices (IEDs). I put together a collection of my explosive ordnance detection (EOD) equipment and several inert IED training aids for show and tell. Getting through airport security with those devices worried me. The security station consisted of a walkthrough metal detector and a table for inspecting packages. I put my bag on the table and walked through the metal detector. I went to open my bag but the inspector just waved me through. I spent four days training the bomb techs. On leaving, I put my case of equipment on the security table and passed through the metal detector. The inspector said, "I don't see an agricultural sticker on your case." Back to the agricultural inspector I went. The agricultural inspector put my case into an x-ray. The screen lit up with all of my inert improvised bombs. The inspector stroked his chin and said, "Nope, I don't see any agricultural products in there." He slapped an OK sticker on my bag and I was good to go. Talk about security! Imagine what would happen today.

In early 1978, I was contacted by a representative of the government of Argentina. That eventually led to a first-class ticket to Argentina. When I boarded the airplane, the entire first-class section was occupied. I wound up being the sole coach-class occupant with four stewardesses to serve me for the twelve-hour flight. Damn, I so wish had taken condoms. On leaving the plane, my host handed me a gun. I asked him what I should do with it. He said, "Shoot anyone you feel like shooting."

A week after my arrival, I was taken before the military junta. They immediately told me they were aware of my problems with the FBI but it didn't seem to matter to them. The junta indicated they were in need of counter eavesdropping, eavesdropping, and bomb detection equipment and the training to use it. I had no problem with the counter eavesdropping and bomb detection equipment. However, I was prevented, by law, from selling them eavesdropping devices. I couldn't see how I could manage such a program without living there and I didn't want to do that.

The junta was put in place by a military coup led by Jorge Videla on March 24, 1976. They seized power because of soaring inflation of roughly 300 percent and the unstable economic conditions caused by the Peronists and other subversive and communist groups. The junta seized between 10,000 and 30,000 men, women, and children because of their western Christian values and made them "disappear." Some were jailed without trial, some were simply killed, and others thrown out of airplanes into the Rio de la Plata river. The junta's end came with the Falkland (Malvinas) War, which disgraced the military, enraged the public, and worsened economic conditions. Inflation had reached 900 percent. The public grew tired of the military and they lost power in 1983. The Dirty War ended when Raul Alfonsin took control of the country.

You can't go to Argentina without seeing at least one soccer match. Mine was Boca versus River Place. I was immediately stuck on entering the stadium by the moat around the soccer field and the attack German Shepherds running loose in it. Around the moat was a chain link fence topped with razor ribbon. Serious stuff. I sat at the third level and that alone was frightening. It was so steep, my knees were at the top of the head of the person in front of me. I visually aligned the railing in front of me with the line on the soccer field and when the fans yelled "Boca, Boca, Boca" and stamped their feet, the railing was going up and down four inches! I couldn't wait to get out of there.

CHAPTER EIGHT

My fame spread internationally and in 1974, right after the Yom Kippur War, the government sent me to Egypt to train their various intelligence agencies on my countermeasure equipment. My soon to be friend, former CIA agent Frank Terpil, made all of the arrangements to get me there. It wasn't an easy trip.

Allow me to digress briefly and say a few words about Frank. He was another super patriot. If you talked to him for five minutes, you would swear you had known him all of your life. His accomplishments included personally removing Idi Amin from Uganda then personally removing Jean-Claude Duvalier from Haiti. Next, he flew to Libya and told Muammar Gaddafi to stop killing people. The killing was cut in half. Frank's next project was to act as one of the negotiators for the Arab-Israeli dispute. Shortly after that, the Deep State decided to call him a terrorist. He was arrested in Jamaica and taken to a prison in New York City. When he awoke after his first night's sleep, the cell door was wide open and no one was in the jail. He walked out to the street, took a cab to Virginia, got his passport, and left for Cuba, where he spent his remaining years.

We were supposed to fly into Athens, Greece on the way to Cairo, but were diverted by a bunch of terrorists to a military airstrip in Thessaloniki, Greece.

Four soldiers with AK-47s got on the plane to search for someone or something. During the incident, the stewardess asked if there was anything she could do for me. I said, "Bring me a Cuban cigar, crackers, some caviar, and vodka." She did. Hey, if you gotta go, you might as well go in style! After an hour or so, we were on our way again.

When we got to Cairo, my bag was among the missing. Once I met my host, he took me to a large warehouse where my bag was sitting all by itself in the middle of the room. Terpil had told me to put a thread under the collars of my shirts, which I did; they had all been moved. I was never told what was behind that whole incident.

Thanks to Terpil, I had sold the Egyptian government (CIA) about $55,000.00 worth of countermeasure equipment. My host took me to all of the usual tourist sites. You cannot be overwhelmed by them. He also took me to the ancient city of Mahdi, located some distance from Cairo. As I roamed throughout the deserted city, a warm glow came over me and I thought, *This is where I came from.* Mahdi also has three pyramids, but they are 2,000 years older than the pyramids of Giza. A canal that brought stones to build the pyramids crossed the desert. Several barges sank there with their stone cargo. I found it interesting that Mahdi is 250 feet above any known water source I Egypt. You figure that one out.

One evening, my host took me to a Bedouin tent in what seemed like the middle of the Sahara Desert. We drove in a Mercedes-Benz and the speedometer remained pegged at 120 miles per hour for the whole distance. As we entered the dimly lit tent, a belly dancer was dancing in the middle of a ten-foot square dance floor. The audience surrounded the floor. A three-piece orchestra consisting of a drum, flute, and one stringed instrument provided the music. My host, bodyguard, and I sat on a slightly raised platform. There was a bowl of munchies on the table and I ate a bunch of them. Turned out they were deep-fried goat's eyes. When I put my hand down by my side, a kitten bit me on the end of my now greasy finger. In a knee-jerk reaction, I yanked my arm up and the kitten flew into the darkness of the tent and landed in the middle of the dance floor. Everybody froze, looked up, and wondered where the heck the cat came from. I really hated to leave Egypt but had serious problems with the caste system. I could never treat another human being in that manner.

In the early 1970s, a disheveled man wearing a mismatched jacket and pants and tennis shoes showed up at my door. Thinking he was another unbalanced person, I told him I had some sensitive material on my desk and asked if he would return in an hour. I used that time trying to figure out what to do with him. It was Edwin Duncan, owner and President/Chairman of Northwestern Bank headquartered in North Wilkesboro, North Carolina. He told me he was having security problems at his bank and was afraid the IRS was bugging him. I agreed to train his security officer, Jerry Starr, who in turn purchased some of my countermeasure equipment. Jerry eventually called me from the bank's home base in North Wilkesboro. He asked if I would come to the bank and go through a sweep with him. He instructed me to go to the Baltimore/Washington International (BWI) Airport and a company plane would pick me up and take me to North Carolina. I was impressed. Sure enough, a twin-engine turboprop showed up and ferried me to North Carolina. On landing at their home airport in North Wilkesboro, I noticed the pilot push a button on the instrument panel and the doors of the very *large* hangar ahead slid open. Inside the hangar were at least six beautiful white airplanes, each with the Northwestern Bank logo on the tail. They ranged in size from a four-engine Fairchild turboprop down to a classic Twin Beech. I was very, very impressed but wondered what a small North Carolina bank was doing with all of those airplanes.

As years went by, I learned a great deal about Duncan. He turned out to be a super patriot and used the bank's resources and airplanes to carry gold bullion from the US Treasury to CIA operations in Central and South America, Northern and

South Vietnam, and the Cayman Islands for various covert operations being conducted in those foreign countries. That is why he kept the IRS at bay. In Cayman, Duncan and Jim Bodden, the father of the Cayman Islands, worked together to fund and manage the monies for the Bay of Pigs invasion into Cuba. Duncan built a string of bungalows he named Harbor Heights on the west coast of the island, next to what is now known as the "public beach," to house the Bay of Pigs operatives.

In 1972, I visited Sir Thomas Brodie MBE (Tom got his MBE by disarming sea mines placed by Cuban terrorists around British Navy ships while they were visiting Miami) with the Dade County (Miami) Bomb Squad. After completing my work for Tom and, while passing through the Miami airport concourse, I noticed a banner saying "Fly to the Cayman Islands...$62.00 round trip." Noting I had that much cash in my pocket and that I could get there and back in one day, I grabbed a flight.

As we were landing, I noticed a large Quonset hut on the left with huge letters on it that said CIA. I smiled and thought, *Those guys are never going to leave me alone.* CIA was Cayman Island Airways. They now call themselves Cayman Airways. Once on Cayman, I knew that this was where I wanted to be. On my return trip, I began scuba diving with Bob Soto. In time, I switched to a new company run by one of Soto's dive masters. Several years later, I again switched to a new dive operation that had a dive boat more to my liking. The dive master, Clint Ebanks, and I became very close friends. One day, we got into a conversation about my bomb work. He revealed that when he was a youngster, he and several of his friends were snorkeling in a small lake on the inland side of the main road across from where Laguna del Mar Condominiums once stood. They stumbled upon a huge underwater cache of weapons. He and his friends put a machine gun on each shoulder and marched into town. Word of the incident swiftly reached Jim Bodden, and he knew exactly who to contact to solve the problem: Ed Duncan. Duncan grabbed plans for one of his existing banks, filled in the lake with marle (crushed limestone), and stuck the bank on it. *Some cork!* The bank was put up with such speed there was no time to change the design. It wound up with the drive-in-window on the wrong side (they drive on the left in Cayman).

CHAPTER NINE

Feeling particularly spry one day, I called FBI Director J. Edgar Hoover and told him I manufactured products that may be of interest to him. He promptly invited me to visit him at headquarters. Walking into his office, I immediately noticed that his desk was on a four-inch pedestal and the legs on the sofa in front of the desk had been sawed off. I sat on the arm of the sofa and looked at him eye to eye. I think he liked that. He passed me on to their intelligence support office where I met John Matter. Matter took me to the U.S. Recording Company elsewhere in Washington and explained how to do business with the FBI through that company. Business went along fine until the Omnibus Crime Bill (Title III) was passed in 1968. Upon reading it, I immediately saw that I could not sell to apparent commercial firms such as U.S. Recording. The FBI gave me a rubber stamp that essentially said, "This order complies with the provisions of the Omnibus Crime Bill." Seeing real problems with that arrangement, any eavesdropping equipment ordered through U.S. Recording was delivered directly to the FBI with the invoice going to U.S. Recording.

During one of my many visits to the FBI technical section, I noticed one of my invoices sitting on Special Agent XX's desk and it was marked up a substantial percentage. I thought that was strange but paid no further attention to it.

Built into the Omnibus Crime Bill (Title III) was an automatic five-year review period. In early 1975, investigators Tim Oliphant and Rick Vermeer of the U.S. House Select Committee on Intelligence contacted me. They requested the opportunity to review my files on sales of eavesdropping equipment. Among those files was one labeled "U.S. Recording." When they asked who this was, I told them it was the FBI. I told them about our relationship, the rubber stamp, the incident about the marked-up invoice, and my confusion about that markup. They requested I prepare a statement detailing my observations on the effectiveness of the Omnibus Crime Bill. I prepared a statement primarily asking why Audio Intelligence Devices (AID), a Florida based manufacturer of eavesdropping equipment, was permitted to inventory and market "off the shelf" equipment while I could not. After my statement was prepared, I contacted the CIA and FBI to see if there were any problems with my appearing before the committee. The FBI made no comment. The CIA asked for a day's delay (a huge snowstorm saw to that) and then gave me the OK. The statement was turned over to the investigators and a day was set for my appearance before the committee.

Upon taking a seat to read my prepared statement, to my astonishment, it had been completely rewritten. The new statement attacked the FBI and made no mention whatsoever of AID. I immediately told Vermeer that I was *not* going to read his statement. He instructed me to go to an anteroom and repair whatever I felt was needed. Not anticipating this level of deception, I had not brought a copy of my original statement. If I had, I most certainly would have read that instead. Given little time to repair a non-repairable statement, I did the best I could. When I read the revised statement, all of the congressmen looked at each other, me, and the paper in front of them, wondering what was happening. To this day, I do not know which of the three statements was read into the congressional record and, quite frankly, I don't give a damn.

On returning to my office, I telephoned FBI Director Kelly (he replaced Hoover, who had died) and requested a meeting with him. Two other high-level FBI officials were present. I would later read the internal FBI communications about that meeting. One of the men wanted to seriously deal with the U.S. Recording problem while the other wanted to execute me on the spot.

Shortly afterward, two FBI agents showed up at my plant and tried to get me to withdraw my testimony. Every half hour, one agent would leave the room to go to the "bathroom," i.e., change the tape in his recorder. He didn't even have the common sense to flush the toilet that was on the other side of the wall from my office to cover his activities. They tried to force me to sign their statement. I initially refused, but later agreed to sign it with the statement "I have *partially* prepared the above statement." That got them out the door.

Shortly after that incident, a "private detective" called and asked if I would show him how to three-wire a telephone. We met in a conference room at a local motel in Towson, Maryland. He handed me a screwdriver and I handed it right back to him. I told him if he wanted to learn the process, *he* would have to do the work. About that time, I noticed the toes of a pair of wing-tipped shoes at the bottom of the curtain that separated the room. Finally, that person entered the room and, along with the other, tried to force me to make the modifications. I declined and departed. What a bunch of nonsense.

In a few weeks, just about every common criminal in the Baltimore area began showing up at my building. None got in the door. The FBI must have informed these scumbags they were being wiretapped by the FBI and Kaiser could fix their problems. This type of nonsense went on for *years*.

63

In the midst of all the various intelligence agencies efforts to do me in, I received a warning from a credible agency friend that the government was going to charge me with an unspecified crime. That warning resulted in this letter to Attorney General Levi.

MARTIN L. KAISER, INC.
Countersurveillance . Bomb Detection .
Surveillance Electronics

March 23, 1976
Hon. Edward Levi
Attorney General of the United States
Department of Justice
Washington, DC.

Dear Mr. Attorney General:

It is with great hesitation that I write to you, however, I believe that I am in serious trouble and that you are the only person who will be able to assist me.

For over ten years, Martin L. Kaiser, Inc. has been a major supplier of electronic countermeasure, surveillance and clandestine bomb detection equipment to law enforcement agencies from the federal level downward. Among my customers, and these but a few, were the CIA, Department of Defense, FBI, State Department, Army, Navy and Air Force Intelligence, Coast Guard, etc. In June, 1975, the National Wiretap Commission, operating under a Congressional mandate, viewed my business records under threat of subpoena. These records were subsequently brought to the attention of the House Select Committee on Intelligence by the National Wiretap Commission. As a result, it became publicly known that the FBI purchased its electronic countermeasure and surveillance equipment through a front known as the U.S. Recording Company. This disclosure has been of extreme embarrassment to the FBI, but I can assure you it is not an embarrassment of my making. I am sure you are well aware of the media's treatment of subsequent events.

Since this fact became known, my business has fallen to virtually zero. No federal agency or, for that matter, local agency will even discuss purchases of equipment with me. I can only assume, but cannot conclusively prove, that the FBI has "passed the word." It is not however, this event and the subsequent economic loss which are of primary concern, for I do engage in other business activities which will carry me through this trying time. Recently, a person of known reliability has pointedly warned me that I am to be made a test case under the criminal wiretap provisions of the 1968 Omnibus Crime Act. Being thoroughly familiar with the complicated and often conflicting provisions of that Act, I am fully aware of the danger existing to anyone who has committed themselves to the manufacture of electronic surveillance equipment.

I have never knowingly violated and have always strictly insisted on compliance with the provisions of the Omnibus Bill. I am firmly convinced that I am not presently violating the Bill, either. However, because of its complexity, my vulnerability, the FBI's pique, the new media's pressure, and the warning relayed to me, quite frankly, I am indeed worried. Although I know full well, based on previous attempts to receive clarification of the Bill, it is not the normal business of the Justice Department to give a "clean bill of health" to a citizen, I indeed wonder if there would be some way for you to advise me whether, under the wildest stretch of imagination, I am contravening any provision of the Omnibus Bill. Although I am reconciled to being driven out of this business, I desperately hope that I will not have to go through a trial in the process.

As mentioned previously, I also manufacture clandestine bomb detection equipment, again, having done this for federal and local agencies. Through a rather lengthy chain of events, the FBI now heads the National Bomb Program. Attempts to contact the FBI immediately after the LaGuardia explosion (which occurred well after my Congressional testimony) resulted in the most callous response I have ever received to one of my offers of assistance. The implications are hideous and further support my desire to resolve the issues as promptly as possible.

As a citizen who has consistently demonstrated his support of the law enforcement community and, therefore, his country, I need your help. Any assistance will be sincerely appreciated.

Respectfully,

Martin L. Kaiser
President

MLK:nre

I sent this letter hoping something would come of it but I received no answer.

Within months of my testimony before the House Select Committee on Intelligence, my business of manufacturing eavesdropping and countermeasure equipment did indeed fall to *zero*. Fortunately, I had the ability to shift into the manufacture of bomb detection and disposal equipment, a marketplace the intelligence community couldn't and wouldn't dare try to control. Heh, heh, was I wrong—again!

Compounding my problems was a series of events that started in mid-1974. Lt. Col. Bob Doms showed up at my door with an armful of pictures and certificates and offered to sell my products. Although I felt uncomfortable with his unannounced approach, I thought I'd give him a try. I used an IBM copy machine and had to report Monday mornings the number of copies made. One Monday, I noticed that roughly 1,200 copies had been made. Since neither my secretary nor I had made them, they obviously were made by Doms. Doms had a booming Amway business, so I assumed he must have made copies of sales brochures. I let him go after two months of no progress. I later learned from my good friend, ex-CIA agent Marshall Soghoian, that he had copied all of my invoices and incoming purchase orders. Shortly after his departure, I learned he was already on the payroll of my Florida-based arch competitor Audio Intelligence Devices (AID). He would later give copies of my records to the House Select Committee on Intelligence that I had appeared before. That infuriated the intelligence community because those documents gave the Select Committee an open window into the technical capabilities of just about every intelligence agency in the country.

Even though it is slightly out of place time wise, I'm putting the Lou Panos *Evening Sun* article next. Events from roughly 1975 onward attach to the FBI criminal case and I'll pick up there.

The Evening Sun
Baltimore, MD
Monday, October 25, 1976
Witness's Business Suddenly Drops

When the House Select Committee on Intelligence invited Marty L. Kaiser to testify at its hearings on illegal wiretapping by government agencies, he did the statesmen a favor and accepted the invitation.

Now they can return it by helping him answer a question: Why is it that he averaged about $200,000 annual in business from these agencies before he testified just one year ago and has averaged zilch since then?

That's what has happened to Martin Kaiser since he went to Washington last October and startled the intelligence community. He offered evidence that prices for equipment he had sold to an FBI front had apparently been marked up by about 30 per cent before delivery from the front to the FBI.[2]

Word later came that Edward H. Levi, Attorney General, ordered an investigation of links between several top echelon FBI officials and the head of the firm serving as the original recipient of the equipment.

Lou Panos of the *The Baltimore Sun* wrote this article about me.

Citizen Kaiser is the slightly stout little fellow from Timonium who has been called "the Michelangelo of electronics" because of his uncanny talent for making things out of juiced up wires and finding such things made by others to bug their fellow man. There was a time when his marvelous little devices—all assembled by his nimble brain and nimble fingers in a small block building next to Brooks Robinson's sporting goods shop—were the rage of the FBI, Secret Service, armed forces and private customers in the world of the super-duper snoop and counter-snoop. His developments in electronic eavesdropping for law enforcement and government intelligence had made him one of the most widely publicized and sought-after specialists in the field.

His equipment and techniques led to the discovery that bugs had been placed on telephones in the offices of Governor Mandel, at least four other governors, and Milton A. Allen, the Supreme Bench judge who was then state's attorney for Baltimore.

---

2   Lou Panos, "Witness's Business Suddenly Drops," *The Evening Sun*, October 25, 1976.

The big, red car in his driveway is known as his "President Sadat Cadillac" because he bought it after a lucrative service performed for the Egyptian chief, training his aides in electronic counterintelligence.

Such foreign work and private assignments like countering industrial espionage, says Marty Kaiser, have enabled his company to survive the withdrawal of government business.

"I'm still busy, but most of my business comes from other sources," he says. "I've tried to find out why I was dropped so suddenly. After all, I didn't ask to talk to the committee. They invited me and made it clear that I'd be subpoenaed if I didn't accept the invitation.

"I even went over and talked to (FBI Director) Clarence Kelley about it for an hour. I was only doing my duty, which is something the FBI certainly ought to understand, and he certainly seemed to understand.

At one-point Citizen Kaiser brought suit against officials of several intelligent and military agencies under the Freedom of information Act in an attempt to get an official reason for his freeze-out.

"About the only thing I got out of that was word from the Army that they have no file on me. I told that they must have, became I was in the Army once. I even gave them my service number, but they said my file must have burned up in a fire at the records center.

For Martin Kaiser, who is more at home in the microcosmic world of transistors and printed circuits than the mystical world of Washington politics, there is something familiar about it all.

Shortly before establishing his Timonium business 12 years ago, he had helped develop a missile detection system heralded in 1964 by President Johnson using the bending beam principle in a device "seeing" beyond the horizon.

At the time, he says, he was making about $6,300.00 a year for Radio Corporation of America after starting at

$3,900.00 about six years earlier. For his sterling work, he was rewarded with an assignment as manager of the anti-missile

project when it was moved from Burlington, Mass., to Barbados, West Indies. But one day, be recalls, an Air Force officer asked him to compare RCA's efforts with Raytheon in similar work. "After evaluating their work against RCA, I really felt they were doing a far better job, really outstanding. I said so, and the next thing we knew was Raytheon had the project.

"I wasn't fired, because that wasn't the way they operate instead, they offered me a promotion—in Australia. I said it was okay if they'd pay to move my wife and kids, too, but they said no, I'd have to pay. I calculated the costs and they came to roughly $14,000 [1963 dollars]. I didn't take the promotion."

There is something faintly similar between the Australia to which Martin Kaiser was to be assigned in 1964 for his compulsive candor with an Air Force officer and the Siberia of the intelligence world to which he has been relegated for speaking out before the House Select Committee on Intelligence in 1975.

For a man whose equipment may form the heart of the nation's defense and counterintelligence system, he seems to be getting short shrift. The least the committee owes him in return for his service is a little help in determining why.

Sometimes, I smile when I think of the comparison to Michelangelo. In reality, what the United States government had done was equivalent to giving me a bucket of white paint and a brush and telling me to paint the white line down the middle of the interstate *while traffic is flowing*.

Obviously, I did *not* have a huge intelligence organization at my disposal, so I did the best I could to uncover those who were libeling and slandering me. I filed numerous suits under the Freedom of Information Act but, unfortunately, that was a total waste of time and money. Here is a good example. Note the date of my request and note the date of the response.

Central Intelligence Agency

Washington, D.C. 20505
14 March *1984*

Mr. Martin Luther Kaiser III
115 Bosley Avenue Cockeysville,
MD 21030 Dear

Mr. Kaiser:

This is in response to your attorney's letter, dated 29 September *1976* in which he appealed on your behalf the decision of this Agency, dated 8 July 1976, regarding your request for all Agency records which may exist concerning you. While two documents have been released to you, we have informed you that we would not grant further access to any documents, if additional documents did exist, that might be responsive to your request.

Your appeal has been presented to the Central Intelligence Agency Information Review Committee. Pursuant to the authority under paragraph 1900.51(a) of Chapter XIX, Title 32 of the code of Federal Regulations, I, as Deputy Director for Administration have determined that the fact of the existence or nonexistence of any documents which would reveal a confidential or covert connection with or interest in matters relating to those set forth in your request is classified pursuant to the appropriate Executive order. Further, I have determined that the fact of the existence or nonexistence of such documents

71

would relate directly to information concerning sources and methods which the Director of Central Intelligence has the responsibility to protect from unauthorized disclosure in accordance with subsection 102 (d) (3) of the National Security Act of 1947 and section 6 of the CIA Act of 1949.

Accordingly, pursuant to Freedom of Information Act (FOIA) exemptions (b)

(1) and (b) {3) respectively, and Privacy Act (PA) exemptions (j) (1) and (k)

(1), your appeal is denied to the extent that it concerns any such documents. By this statement we are neither confirming nor denying that such documents exist.

Material withheld under FOIA exemption (b) (1) encompasses matters which are specifically authorized under criteria established by the appropriate Executive order to be kept secret in the interest of national defense or foreign policy and which are in fact currently and properly classified. Exemption (b) (3) pertains to information exempt from disclosure by statute. The relevant statutes are subsection 102 (d) (3) of the National Security Act of 1947, as amended, 50 U.S.C. 403 (d) (3) which makes the Director of Central Intelligence responsible for protecting intelligence sources and methods from unauthorized disclosure, and section 6 of the Central Intelligence Agency Act of 1949, as amended, 50

U.S.C. 403g, which exempts from the disclosure requirement information pertaining to the organization, functions, names, official titles, salaries or numbers of personnel employed by the Agency.

Material withheld on the basis of PA exemption (j) (1) concerns intelligence sources and methods encompassed by those portions of systems of records which the Director of Central Intelligence has determined to be exempt from access by individuals pursuant to the authority granted by this sub-section and regulations promulgated thereunder (32 C.F.R. 1901.61). Information withheld on the basis of exemption (k) (1) in this instance encompasses those portions of all systems of records which the Director of Central Intelligence has determined to be exempt from access by individuals pursuant to the authority granted by this subsection and regulations promulgated thereunder (32 C.F.R. 1901.71) because the material is properly classified under the terms of the appropriate Executive order and subject to the provisions of Section 552(b) (1) of the Freedom of Information Act, as amended.

In accordance with the provisions of the Freedom of Information Act and the privacy Act you have the right to seek judicial review of the above determinations in a United States district court.

We regret that our response to your letter of appeal has been so long delayed and that we cannot be of further assistance to you in this matter.

Sincerely,

Harry E. Fitzwater
Chairman
Information Review Committee (emphasis added)

My success was, as you can see, limited. It wasn't until after my criminal trial that I uncovered one of the documents that provided the driving source for the incessant anger against me. As a Christian, I found it difficult to believe that some individuals would continue a vendetta for such a long period of time, yet, it was true. The vendetta continues to this day (2024).

The picture is of me (far right) at the congressional hearings. In front of me are the 1040 countermeasure kit and Cushman spectrum analyzer.

The US Recording Scandal

Here is Attorney General Levi's report on the U.S. Recording scandal that Mr. Panos and I are referring to. Read it and weep.

STATEMENT BY ATTORNEY GENERAL GRIFFIN B. BELL ON THE RELEASE OF THE U.S. RECORDING REPORT

I am today releasing a report on an investigation of allegations that certain individuals misused their official positions while employed by the Federal Bureau of Investigation. After careful consideration, I decided to issue a full public report.

When reporting on disciplinary actions taken against government employees, federal agencies have traditionally made public the administrative action taken and the nature of the conduct which caused the action to be taken, but have not always identified the particular individuals involved.

There are, however, certain instances of employee misconduct which call into question the integrity of the institution itself. If the agency's mission is particularly sensitive, the misconduct serious, or the officials of high rank, then the public interest is best served by more extensive disclosure.

It is this kind of wrongdoing which is described in the report I am releasing.

In cases such as this one, personal privacy considerations must give way to the legitimate interest of the American public in knowing how its government operates and how high-ranking officials have abused their official positions and neglected their official responsibilities.

High-ranking officials entrusted with public office simply cannot expect the same measure of privacy about the way they perform their official duties or use their offices as they could expect if they were private citizens. Moreover, the public has a legitimate interest in knowing and being able to evaluate how the heads of Executive agencies deal with official misconduct and take corrective action to ensure that similar, abuses of power and position do not recur. In this particular instance, it is my judgment that the public is entitled to know which officials engaged in the misconduct and which officials did not.

The misconduct summarized here, and reports in the news media about these allegations, have cast a shadow over a great institution and over those of its officials who engaged in no wrongdoing whatsoever. I am vitally interested in restoring public confidence in the Federal Bureau of Investigation. This report will confirm that very few individuals engaged in improper conduct. We should bear in mind that this small number of individuals in no way represents the thousands of FBI employees who are dedicated, honest public servants and whose personal and professional integrity is beyond reproach.

Today I asked Director Kelley to issue a bulletin to all Bureau officials in which it will be made clear that neither the Department of Justice nor the FBI as institutions, nor I, as Attorney General, will tolerate the kind of misuse of office or abuse of authority described in this report. I am pleased to note that Director Kelley has made the following structural reforms to prevent the recurrence of the kind of improper practices described in this report:

1. Reorganized the Inspection Division and renamed it the Planning and Inspection Division;' created the Office of Professional Responsibility, an Office of Inspections, and an Office of Planning and Evaluation; established within the Office of Inspections a separate Audit Unit, responsible for auditing all FBI funds and financial transactions; and organized the Division so that it reports directly to him, as Director.

2. Removed the Property Procurement and Management Section from the Division with budget responsibility, the Finance and Personnel Division, thereby making one Division head responsible for procurement and another responsible for the FBI budget and funds. Director Kelley has placed a Special Agent Accountant, a Certified Public Accountant, as Section Chief of the Property Procurement and Management Section.

3. Discontinued the use of the U. S. Recording Company as a "cover" or "cutout" for confidential purposes and established controls to ensure that all purchases are made in accordance with government regulations.

4. Restructured the FBI inventory system, to provide built-in controls and audit trails, and initiated automation of the inventory system to provide better accountability.

5. Discontinued the FBI Laboratory and Exhibits Sections' practice of providing personal services to FBI officials. Director Kelley also has discontinued the use of the unauthorized cash fund once maintained in the Exhibits Section.

6. Reorganized the management and handling of the FBI Recreation Association (FBIRA) and its funds, so that FBIRA officers are aware of their responsibilities to prevent unauthorized expenditures. A new Treasurer of the FBIRA has taken office and is not responsible for any other FBI fund.

7. Replaced the FBI Confidential Fund with the Field Support Account, an imprest fund approved by the Treasury Department.

8. Developed and improved the FBI career development program for Special Agents to ensure that the best qualified individuals are selected for administrative advancement, substantially reducing the possibility that one person or group can control the selection of such candidates. In addition, Director Kelley assures me that the FBI has taken other steps to prevent the kind of misconduct described here. The Bureau has increased legal instruction within its training curriculum; held training sessions on the FBI guidelines for career agents; and issued detailed instructions to the field on legal questions concerning the legality and propriety of investigative techniques. In connection with the latter step, the FBI is seeking advice from the Department's Office of Legal Counsel with increasing frequency.

I have asked Director Kelley to bring to my attention any improper attempts to have FBI agents conduct investigations or undertake activities which are not within the Bureau's authorized jurisdiction. I have directed all Bureau personnel to bring reports of misconduct to the attention of appropriate Bureau officials and, when necessary, the Office of Professional Responsibility at the Bureau and Office of Professional Responsibility here at the Justice Department.

Recognizing the concern of Bureau personnel about threatened civil litigation we have submitted legislation to the Congress which would protect FBI personnel against civil suits by substituting the government as defendant. I believe this approach will protect the rights of citizens without unfairly penalizing individual agents.

The release of this summary report is intended to assure the nation that the Justice Department can investigate and police itself. It will also put all officials of this Department on notice that they will be held accountable to the American people for the manner in which they discharge their official responsibilities while employed as servants of the American people.

THE DEPARTMENT OF JUSTICE REPORT ON THE RELATIONSHIP BETWEEN UNITED STATES RECORDING COMPANY AND THE FEDERAL BUREAU OF INVESTIGATION AND CERTAIN OTHER MATTERS PERTAINING TO THE F.B.I. JANUARY, 1978

This is a report on a Department of Justice investigation of alleged misconduct by certain past and present officials of the Federal Bureau of Investigation.

In the Fall of 1975, the House Select Committee on Intelligence provided the Department with information that certain officials of the F.B.I. were allegedly profiting from the Bureau's business transactions with its exclusive electronics equipment supplier, the United States Recording Company of Washington, D.C. On November 3, 1975, Attorney General Edward H. Levi requested F.B.I. Director Clarence M. Kelley to investigate these allegations. Director Kelley appointed an Ad Hoc Committee to oversee an inquiry by the F.B.I.'s Inspection Division, the Bureau unit ordinarily responsible for internal investigations. Attorney General Levi found the report of the Inspection Division and the Ad Hoc Committee to be incomplete and unsatisfactory. On January 2, 1976, he directed the office of Professional Responsibility and the Criminal Division to review the Inspection Division Report and conduct an independent investigation. The Deputy Attorney General requested two Criminal Division attorneys to work with the office of Professional Responsibility in supervising a special team of F.B.I. investigators, who were carefully selected from Bureau field offices for their ability and experience. I.R.S. agents were also selected to investigate the tax implications of the allegations.

Hundreds of past and present F.B.I. officials were interviewed.

Agent accountants examined vast quantities of documents and records to determine the nature of the F.B.I. U.S.R.C. relationship and the FBI's procedures for purchasing electronic equipment. As the investigation proceeded and possible criminal violations emerged, a Federal Grand Jury in the District of Columbia, raided by the Criminal Division attorneys, began to review the findings of the Department's investigators.

The investigation was completed on November 11, 1976. The findings went beyond the original allegations into other areas of misconduct uncovered by the investigation. The Criminal Division investigative report examined the use of Government material and personnel services by F.B.I. officials for their personal benefit; the administrative mishandling and misapplication of appropriated funds; the misuse of funds of the FBI Recreation Association—a private association of FBI employees; and improprieties in FBI's the dealings with contractors other than USRC.Joseph Tait has been owner and manager of the United States Recording Company (USRC) since 1938. Incorporated in 1969 in the District of Columbia, USRC sells and distributes electronic equipment, principally to the Federal Government. Mr. Tait started doing business with the Government in 1943, when Army Intelligence asked the Bureau's Laboratory Division, then interested in purchasing two Army microphones, to use USRC as a middleman. In the late 1940's, USRC contracted with the Bureau to service amplifiers, recorders and other technical equipment used by the Laboratory Division. From 1963 to 1975, USRC was virtually the sole supplier of electronic equipment to the FBI, and bureau purchase orders were frequently directed to USRC without open bidding as required by Government procurement statutes and regulations._1/

FBI officials justified the exclusive relationship under a specific exemption for purchases that require confidentiality for security reasons._2/

The following facts do not support this explanation, however. For instance, from 1971 to 1975, the Bureau made $500,000 worth of exclusive purchases from USRC which were not marked as confidential. Much of the equipment, including transmitters, receivers, and microphones, clearly fell into the "sensitive" category, but it was not clear why other "nonsensitive" equipment was purchased exclusively from USRC. Also, the Bureau took few precautions to insure the security and confidentiality of the FBI-USRC relationship. A number of electronic equipment manufacturers and suppliers were aware that the FBI used USRC as a middleman. The Bureau often purchased equipment directly from the manufacturer, but always paid its bills through USRC. USRC employees did not receive security clearances. The firm was broken into on at least two occasions. USRC made equipment deliveries to the FBI during working hours in a panel truck plainly marked "U.S. Recording Company."

Moreover, the FBI failed to follow proper procedures for such "confidential" purchases. Section 252(c)(12) of Title 41 of the United States Code requires an agency head to make a determination that the purchase of certain equipment should not be publicly disclosed before public advertising and open bidding regulations can be suspended. ado evidence was found that either the Attorney General or the FBI Director ever made such a formal determination. The procurement regulations were also evaded, and the scrutiny of the Department of Justice avoided, by the "splitting" of orders to USRC so that no single order exceeded $2,500, the limit above which all purchase orders had to be advertised for open bid._3/

From 1961 to 1973, the Bureau purchased large quantities of tape recorders, playback units, closed circuit television systems, video tape machines, laboratory test equipment and FM radio equipment under confidential contract with USRC to the virtual exclusion of all other contractors. The costs to the Government of this special relationship were considerable. From Fiscal Year 1971 through 1975, 60 percent of USRC's total sales were made to the Bureau.

Department investigators examined 1,339 USRC sales invoices, compared the cost of each item, where available, to USRC to the price USRC charged the Bureau, and found an average markup of 23.8 percent from Fiscal Year 1969 through 1975. Individual markups varied widely and were as high as 40 to 70 percent. In addition to high markups, by using USRC as a middleman, the Bureau was not able to purchase equipment at discount prices offered by manufacturers for direct sales on large orders. For example, in 1971 the Bureau paid USRC $147,261.50 for burglar alarm equipment which could have been purchased from a New York supplier for $81,357.00.

USRC asserted that its overhead costs amounted to 15 to 16 percent over the price it paid to the manufacturer. Department investigators found no objective evidence supporting a figure this high.

These findings essentially confirmed allegations made by a Special Agent of the FBI's Radio Engineering Section in 1973. He reported that the FBI paid too much for USRC equipment, that USRC markups were too high, that FBI employees were forced to buy inexpensive items from USRC when they were available elsewhere, and that the FBI-USRC relationship was not confidential. An Inspection Division inquiry was made into those allegations, but this investigation found that during that inquiry key witnesses were not interviewed. One Bureau official, now retired, provided Inspection Division investigators with palpably inaccurate information. The committees which reviewed the inquiry recommended the continued use of USRC as a "cutout" (i.e. a middleman used to conceal the Bureau's identity from outsiders) for confidential procurement without any sound basis for the conclusion. The agent who made the complaint was denied promotion and then transferred to the Tampa Field office, where the Special Agent-in-Charge was told the agent was not a good "team" player and did not get along with other employees.

The officials chiefly responsible for the proper implementation of procurement requirements and procedures were John P. Mohr, Assistant to the Director for Administrative Affairs; Nicholas P. Callahan, Assistant Director, Administrative Division; and G. Speights McMichael, Chief Procurement Officer. The investigation clearly established that these officials knowingly failed to apply required procurement procedures to purchases from USRC. Two possible motives were found for their actions.

No evidence of cash kickbacks or bribes was discovered. Rather, a pattern of social contacts and minor gratuities was revealed between Mr. Tait and various FBI officials, including Messrs. Mohr, Callahan and McMichael. In the 1960's, Mr. Tait and a number of high Bureau officials would get together at the Blue Ridge Rod and Gun Club (Blue Ridge Club)_4/ to play poker. The poker parties would begin on Friday evening and continue until Saturday noon. (Each participant paid the host, a Bureau official, for the cost of food and lodging.)

Mr. Tait also entertained FBI officials on occasion at the Bethesda Country Club, Billy Martin's Carriage House in Georgetown, and the Rotunda Restaurant on Capitol Hill. There was no evidence of excessive drinking, associating with the opposite sex, payoffs, big winners or losers. Nor was there evidence that official FBI files were destroyed, as alleged, at the Blue Ridge Club.

Mr. Tait often gave Laboratory Division employees small gifts at Christmas time, such as tie clasps, wallets, manicure sets, and desk calendars. In 1971, Mr. Tait gave one FBI employee a stereo playback unit for his car after he retired from the Bureau. A former USRC employee stated that in 1969 Mr. Tait purchased and paid for the installation of an eight track tape player with two speakers in John P. Mohr's Cadillac at a total cost of $172.12. There was no other evidence of any personal benefit to any other FBI official.

The investigation also disclosed another possible reason for the Bureau's special relationship with Mr. Tait and USRC. Over the years, Bureau officials came to trust. Tait's willingness to keep the FBI-USRC relationship confidential, and especially, to keep Congress in the dark about FBI eavesdropping practices. In a March 14, 1963, memorandum to Laboratory Assistant Director, Ivan W. Conrad, M. Mohr ordered that.no recorders are to be purchased by the Bureau outside of USRC. The reason for this is because Mr. Tait of USRC will protect the Bureau in the event questions are asked by a Congressional committee concerning the purchase of recorders by the FBI. Other companies will not do this for the Bureau.

On May 22, 1964, after learning that Mr. Tait had been invited to testify before the Senate Subcommittee on Administrative Practice and Procedure, Mr. Mohr wrote in a memorandum:

...Mr. Tait told me he does not know at this point just what he is going to do with the letter but he does not intend to furnish the Subcommittee with any specific information. It should be noted that the Bureau purchases virtually all of its electronic eavesdropping devices from the U.S. Recording Company. Over the years bite. Tait has been an excellent friend of the Bureau and would go to any lengths to protect our interests from any sources. He is a personal friend of mine and he told me that he would most certainly furnish us with any response that he makes to the Subcommittee's letter before submitting it to the Subcommittee._5/

According to past and present employees of the Radio Engineering Section, Mr. Mohr's March 1963 order initiated the Bureau's exclusive relationship with USRC.

The Department concluded that FBI officials showed an improper favoritism to Mr. Tait and USRC in violation of specific conflict of interest regulations of the Department of Justice._-6/

However, no evidence was found indicating a fraudulent intent sufficient to make out a crime under Federal bribery or fraud statutes.

B. Tax Investigation

Mr. Tait was tried and, on June 20, 1977, acquitted of all tax evasion charges under Title 26, United States Code, Section 7201, for the years 1971, 1972 and 1973.

The Department found no evidence that Mr. Mohr violated any federal tax laws.

C. Conversion of Electronic Equipment

Ivan W. Conrad, former Assistant Director of the FBI Laboratory Division, was found to have taken a large quantity of FBI electronic equipment to his home, principally, between 1964 and 1966. Conrad liked to tinker with electronic equipment and was a "ham" radio operator. The equipment included voltmeters, watt meters, battery testers, stereo amplifiers, consoles, speakers, microphones, cables, sidewinders, mixers, tape recorders, transformers, and other sorts of electronic gadgetry. This equipment was evidently delivered directly from USRC to Mr. Conrad's office at FBI headquarters and he took the equipment home. No record was made on FBI inventory files that Mr. Conrad had possession of the equipment.

In late December 1975, after being questioned by investigators from the 1975 Inspection Division inquiry about unaccounted for equipment and after denying knowledge of it, Mr. Conrad, with Mr. Tait's assistance, shipped twenty-nine packages of electronic recording "ham" radio equipment and a large recording console from his home to the USRC warehouse in Southeast Washington. This included the equipment about which he had been questioned. A USRC employee made the delivery in a USRC truck. As much as eighty percent of the equipment had never been used and was in excellent condition. This equipment was subsequently recovered for the Bureau by this investigation. Purchasing documents revealed an acquisition cost of over $20,000.

Mr. Conrad, who retired in July 1973, was interviewed four times during this investigation. He admitted that the equipment once belonged to the FBI. While head of the Laboratory Division, he ordered the equipment from USRC and then used it on "special projects" for Director Hoover, he said. He serviced the Director's television, hi-fi sets, shortwave radio, and designed a portable recording system for him. The console recorder was delivered directly to his home by Mr. Tait, and he took the other equipment home after USRC delivered it to the Bureau. He said that most of the equipment was obtained between 1964 and 1966.

Mr. Conrad asserted that he never intended to convert this equipment to his own use. After Director Hoover died in 1972, he wanted either to buy the equipment from USRC or return it to the company. He said he was "tardy" in not returning it to Mr. Tait until late December 1975. In August 1976, in response to inquiries from this investigation, he delivered another shipment of electronic equipment to the FBI. He had signed this out of FBI Laboratory stocks in the early 1960's. Auto radios, control cables, heads, speakers, antennas, assorted accessory equipment, a stereo receiver, tape recorders, microphones, and a sound recording set were included in this shipment. It is believed that all FBI equipment that was in Mr. Conrad's possession has now been recovered.

D. Goods and Services of the FBI's Exhibits Section

The Department also investigated the allegation that FBI employees were required to provide goods and services to their superiors. The Exhibits Section of the FBI is staffed with accomplished craftsmen and artisans. Their official task is to design and construct exhibits for use in Department litigation and displays, furniture, and other exhibits for internal FBI use. The Radio Engineering Section is responsible for maintaining and servicing FBI electronic equipment. Interviews with past and present employees of those sections and an examination of photographs and personal logs maintained by some of them revealed that services were provided to FBI officials during official duty hours and that goods were produced for FBI officials with Government property and equipment._7/ This constituted a misuse of Government time and materials, contrary to federal law and regulations. 18 U.S.C. 641; 28 C.F.R.§45.735-16. Prosecutions, where otherwise possible, are barred by the statute of limitations as virtually all of the following misconduct occurred more than five years ago. 18 U.S.C. 3282.

1. Director J. Edgar Hoover

Exhibits Section employees painted Director Hoover's house each year when he visited California during the summer. They built a front portico onto his house and dug a fish pond, equipping it with water pump and outdoor lights. They constructed shelves, telephone stands, and an oriental fruit bowl. Home appliances, air conditioners, stereo equipment, tape recorders, and television sets, and electric wiring were serviced and repaired by Radio Engineering. Section employees. Exhibits Section employees serviced his lawn mower and snow blower, maintained his yard, replaced sod twice a year, installed artificial turf, and planted and moved shrubbery. The Exhibits Section built a deck in the rear of his house, a redwood garden fence, a flagstone court and sidewalks. A power window with sliding glass doors was also designed and constructed. Clocks were reset, metal polished, wallpaper re touched, firewood provided, and furniture rearranged. Employees were on call night and day for this work.

Mr. Hoover employed one grade 15 Bureau accountant to give him tax advice, maintain his tax records, and prepare his annual Federal tax return. His secretary or two associates would generally make the work requests. Exhibits Section employees were called upon to build gifts for Director Hoover every year for Christmas, his service anniversary and other special occasions. These gifts included furniture such as tables, display cases, cabinets, a bar and valets. Assistant Directors chipped in to pay for cost of materials. Employee labor, however, was not compensated.

FBI employees called upon to perform these services did not think them proper, but felt compelled to follow orders for fear of losing their jobs, or of arbitrary transfers or promotion delays.

2. John P. Mohr

Mr. Mohr had car radios repaired, the body of his son's MG repaired and re painted, and an elaborate dental exhibit constructed for his son, a dentist. At his home, Exhibits Section employees shaved doors to accommodate new carpeting, and Radio Engineering Section employees repaired his television numerous times, and installed phones, stereo hi-fi speakers (Mr. Mohr's property) and a burglar alarm system which required frequent servicing after installation (FBI property). They repaired his stereo and purchased and installed a new FM radio tuner in an existing cabinet which was modified by Exhibits Section employees. Mr. Mohr also received certain gifts made by the Exhibits Section, including a coat of arms, a dresser top valet, and an oak portable liquor cabinet in the shape of a wine case.

Exhibits Section employees painted a desk and made a drawing board for Mr. Mohr. They made, at his direction, a walnut cigar box, a walnut tape cartridge rack, a walnut wine rack cabinet whose value has been estimated at $2,000, and two walnut gun cases with glass front doors.

Mr. Mohr had employees mount snow tires, wash, and transport his personal automobile to commercial garages for repairs. A battery was installed in his car and a turn signal lamp was replaced by Exhibits Section employees. Mr. Mohr also received tapes of record albums which were copied and distributed by Radio Engineering Section employees at the direction of former Assistant to the Director Cartha D. DeLoach.

Mr. Mohr received services even after he retired in June 1972. Radio Engineering Section employees were sent to his home, at his request, to repair electrical switches, televisions, and the burglar alarm system which had been installed earlier. Mr. Mohr also asked a Radio Engineering Section employee to repair his electric blood pressure machine. At Mr. Mohr's request to former Exhibits Section Chief John P. Dunphy, the Exhibits Section built a birdhouse according to plans he provided.

3. Nicholas P. Callahan

For Mr. Callahan, Exhibits Section employees silk screened a felt cloth used for table games, cut doors at his house to accommodate new carpeting, printed maps showing the location of his beach home and finished Styrofoam nautical objects to decorate it. They made walnut fishing rod racks for his beach home, assembled a lathe fence to prevent sand erosion at his beach home, and built a picket fence for his residence._8/

He had walnut shelves cut by section employees during official hours (he supplied the material), had a piece of plywood covered with weatherproof material for a shed roof, had Exhibits Section employees make a sign for his daughter and son-in-law with their name, and had former Exhibits Section Chief Leo J. Gauthier make a fuse box cover for the basement recreation room in his home. At his request, the exhibits section cast a desk memento in plastic for him to give to a friend and make him a set of stack tables which duplicated a set which had been made for Director Kelley (see below). Radio Engineering Section employees diagnosed troubles with his televisions and Exhibits Section employees framed his personal photographs.

Mr. Callahan also received various gifts. He received a framed plaque which recited an Irish prayer, a plaque bearing his coat of arms, a dresser top valet, a portable oak liquor cabinet in the shape of a wine cask, a decorative Christmas tree ball and a gold medallion and chain for Mrs. Callahan into which a gold disc with the FBI seal was set by the Exhibits Section (Mr. Callahan bought the medallion and chain). The valet and liquor cabinet were duplicates of gifts given to Director Hoover, Mr. Mohr and Mr. Dunphy.

Mr. Callahan also received considerable services to his automobile.

Employees test drove his personal car, did diagnostic work on it, took it out for washes, fill-ups, snow tire mounting, and servicing at garages and muffler shops. Scratches on his car were touched up. (Some employees, however, recalled that the whole trunk lid on Mr. Callahan's car was painted.)

Mr. Callahan states that Mr. McMichael provided him with a Polaroid camera which he used for personal photographs. Film for the camera was also provided at FBI expense. He has since returned the camera.___9/

4. John P. Dunphy

On August 13, 1976, Mr. Dunphy pleaded guilty to a misdemeanor charge under Section 641, Title 18, United States Code, as part of an agreement with the United States as a result of which he voluntarily tendered his resignation from his position as Chief of the Exhibits Section and cooperated with this investigation.__10/

5. Director Clarence M. Kelley

on directions from Mr. Callahan shortly after Director Kelley and his wife moved to Washington, two sets of valances were made and installed in Director Kelley's apartment by the Exhibits Section and two television sets were purchased and installed by the Radio Engineering

Section. After this investigation began, Director Kelley paid for the estimated cost of the valances. Director Kelley admitted he knew, after the job was done, that the Exhibits Section installed the first set of valances. when they proved unsatisfactory, he requested a second set to be built and installed. This set was also built and installed by Exhibits Section employees. The television sets were ordered returned by Director Kelley after this investigation revealed their source. Although Mr. Callahan said he directed that the televisions be loaned to Director Kelley, the sets were not entered on FBI equipment inventory until after their return from Director Kelley's apartment on February 19, 1976.

The Exhibits Section also built a walnut table, a set of stack tables, and a jewelry box which were given to Director Kelley as gifts from the Executive Conference. He was unaware that the Exhibits Section made the gifts, he said. The Conference, by donations from its members, paid for the materials used in these gifts.

Director Kelley's personal automobile received occasional servicing by FBI employees and his FBI-provided chauffeur performed personal errands for him. Section employees repaired a broken cabinet for Director Kelley, and mounted the FBI seal on a gold disc as a charm for the Director's wife.

6. Miscellaneous

The practice of providing FBI goods and services to high Bureau officials was not limited to the above individuals.

Clyde Tolson, longtime Associate Director under Hoover, had FBI employees develop several patented devices during official hours. These included a reusable bottle cap and a power window opener. These patents were assigned to the FBI. There was no evidence that Mr. Tolson personally benefited from the development of these devices. One of the power windows was installed for President Johnson in the White House.

A second unit, designed and intended for President Johnson's ranch, was never completed.

E. Imprest Fund

There was evidence that an FBI official received reimbursement from the FBI Imprest Fund (petty cash fund) for personal purchases.

G. McMichael, Chief Procurement officer, denied that Imprest Funds were used for the personal purchases of Bureau officials. He stated that he did not check to see whether the purchases were proper. Under Federal law he was required, as the Bureau's chief procurement officer, to certify that each disbursement was proper and correct. Each voucher reads, in part: "I certify that the disbursements claimed herein are correct and proper..."Many of the personal purchases could have been used by the Exhibits Section and, therefore, could have escaped Mr. McMichael's attention. He admitted being derelict in his responsibilities as the Imprest Fund's cashier, disbursing and certifying officer.

F. Confidential Fund

Part of the FBI's annual appropriation is specified "not to exceed $70,000 to meet unforeseen emergencies of a confidential character to be expended under the direction of the Attorney General and to be accounted for solely on his certificate." The most common use is for payments to informants. Contrary to the appropriation language and to Federal regulations, this money was drawn from the Treasury by travel vouchers that failed to reflect the actual expenditures. Top FBI administrative officers were, therefore, able to maintain in cash form these monies over which they exercised custody and control. Field offices were given separate funds for payment of informants which were maintained in separate accounts in addition to the so-called "Confidential Fund" which was kept at headquarters. Also contrary to Federal regulations, the unspent portion of the yearly appropriation was accumulated. By 1974, the headquarters "Confidential Fund" totaled $34,000.

Nicholas P. Callahan controlled the Fund from 1946, when he was Number One man to the Assistant Director of the Administrative Division, until July 1973, when he became Associate Director. John P. Mohr, Clyde Tolson, and Director Hoover could also authorize disbursements. A 1974 inspection of the Fund concluded that "no written guidelines exist pertaining to the utilization of this fund" and that separate records for this fund were kept by FBI administrative units apart from the FBI's normal accounting system and were not subject to Treasury Department audit. This investigation revealed uses of the "Confidential Fund" maintained at headquarters by FBI administrative officers that were not within the scope of the appropriation._12/

This investigation revealed that between August 1956 and May 1973 the Bureau purchased over $75,000 worth of electronic equipment with money from the Confidential Fund. No memoranda, purchase orders, requisitions, vouchers or similar documentation were located indicating why the equipment was purchased or who requested it. Mr. Callahan acknowledged that Mr. Mohr and he decided to use Confidential Fund monies to purchase electronic equipment. This was not done to disguise the nature of the equipment, he said, but to expedite large purchases of equipment.

The Confidential Fund was also used to pay for public relations expenses. Between 1961 and 1975, $23,399.15 of Confidential Funds were spent on room rentals, food, drink and gifts for the liaison officers of foreign and domestic law enforcement and intelligence gathering organizations. Mr. Callahan approved disbursements for liaison functions. There was also evidence that Mr. Mohr, and, to a far lesser extent, Assistant Director Eugene W. Walsh, and Deputy Associate Director Thomas J. Jenkins also authorized such disbursements. Director Kelley recalled such an authorization by himself on one occasion.

One of these officials stated that any expenditure which in any way aids "the detection and prosecution of crimes against the United States," including liaison functions, is justified under the FBI's total appropriation and that the Confidential Fund was used only to expedite reimbursement. He admitted, however, that the Confidential Fund had been obtained on the representation to Treasury that they would be used for "unforeseen emergencies of a confidential character." Congress had not been informed that the Bureau was incurring public relations and liaison expenses and paying them out of the Confidential Fund. The Bureau had never submitted a formal request to Congress or the Office of Management and Budget for the proper budget authority to make these Confidential Fund expenditures. Title 31, United States Code, Section 551, which prohibits the use of appropriated funds for lodging, feeding, or providing transportation to an assemblage, can be interpreted specifically to prohibit the use of the Confidential Fund for public relations and liaison purposes.

This investigation also revealed that FBI officials used the Confidential Fund to cash personal checks. This practice was stopped after Mr. Welsh was questioned about the practice on May 21, 1976.

No evidence was found indicating that any senior official applied these appropriated funds to his own use.

G. The FBI Recreation Association

The FBI Recreation Association (FBIRA) was founded in 1931 for the purpose of promoting and encouraging athletic, social and welfare activities among its members. The FBIRA is an independent and tax-exempt organization whose membership is voluntary. The Association's funds were spent on athletic and social functions, group travel, clubs, hobbies, art shows, and publication of The Investigator, a monthly magazine reporting on FBIRA activities. Its constitution and bylaws provide for the election of officers and a five-member Board of Directors.

This investigation revealed that between September 1951 and June 1972, Nicholas P. Callahan obtained $39,590.98 from the FBIRA designated for the "Library Fund." The Association's records contain no explanation or authorization for these disbursements. No disbursement requests or vouchers were found. Mr. Callahan was the Library Fund's only recipient and maintained the only records of its expenditures. Mr. Mohr periodically reviewed the records.

Shortly after Mr. Hoover died, Mr. Callahan and Mr. Mohr discontinued the Fund and destroyed its records. Neither of the two FBIRA treasurers who served during this period knew why the fund was named the Library Fund in the FBIRA Disbursements Journal. The treasurers understood that these "Library Fund" disbursements were for Director Hoover's public relations expenses, such as office flowers, condolence telegrams, and for unspecified office expenses, such as books and newspapers.

Only Messrs. Hoover, Tolson, Callahan, Mohr, and the treasurers knew about the "Library Fund" and disbursements were made to the Fund without the authorization of FBI-RA officers whose approval is required under the FBIRA charter. Mr. Callahan asserted that the disbursements were for official public relations and liaison functions for which appropriated funds are unavailable under law and that they were proper under a broad interpretation of the FBIRA constitution's "general welfare" clause because money spent promoting the FBI's general welfare is in the best interest of its employees.

The investigation also revealed that $55,849.77 of FBIRA funds were expended on receptions for National Academy students and guests between April 8, 1958, and June 20, 1972. The National Academy is an FBI operated training and education facility for local law enforcement personnel around the country. The receptions were not FBIRA activities and they were not open to FBIRA members. About half the cost of the receptions was borne by those attending the receptions so that net cost to the FBIRA after offset by these donations was $29,443.67. The FBIRA constitution and bylaws do not provide for expenditures for such functions as National Academy receptions.

From July 1952 to December 1975, another $12,219.90 of FBIRA funds were spent on miscellaneous or liaison expenses and on receptions, luncheons, retirement parties, and gifts for foreign law enforcement liaison officers, and senior FBI officials. The funds also covered the cost of FBI press receptions and other public relations expenses. Director Hoover, Mr. Callahan, Mr. Mohr, Mr. DeLoach, and Mr. Walsh, not the FBIRA Board of Directors, approved these disbursements, according to the records.

The above facts established that, from 1951 to 1975, high officials of the FBI obtained funds from the FBIRA for public relations and other uses not authorized by its charter and without obtaining the approval of its Board of Directors. There is no evidence that these Bureau officials converted the money to their own use and, therefore, no evidence of criminal intent as required under Title 18, United States Code, Section 654.

H. Special Agents Mutual Benefit Association (SAMBA)

SAMBA is an unincorporated association designed to provide life and health insurance to FBI employee members. The Prudential Insurance Company has been SAMBA's underwriter since SAMBA was founded in 1948. SAMBA is independent of the FBI, with private offices at 1325 G Street, N.W., Washington, D.C.

This investigation uncovered questionable expenses from SAMBA books and records. The amount of $635.21 was withdrawn from the SAMBA account to pay for a retirement party and gift for Mr. Mohr. $310.22 of this withdrawal covered the price of a Sears Roebuck fishing boat, which was delivered to Mr. Mohr by FBI employees. One SAMBA officer admitted that SAMBA funds were used, in disregard of its charter, to pay for retirement parties, luncheons, and gifts for outgoing SAMBA officials and Directors. Other questionable expenses included two professional football season tickets for the use of a SAr4BA official, Saturday work charges, wedding and anniversary gifts, and annual Christmas parties. Director Kelley and his wife, along with Mr. and Mrs. Mohr, Mr. and Mrs. Thomas Jenkins, and SAMBA President Thomas J. Feeney, Jr., and his wife, attended a weekend meeting in New York City with officials of Prudential Life Insurance Company, which underwrites the SAMBA policy. Director Kelley's travel from Kansas City, Missouri, to New York and return to Washington, D.C., was by Government Travel Request (GTR). Travel for Mrs. Kelley and the others was paid by SAMBA. Prudential paid all other expenses. Director Kelley subsequently reimbursed Prudential for these expenses.

I. FBI Officials' Relations with Firearms Suppliers

The Remington Arms Company, which bids on arms and ammunition contracts with the FBI, maintains a 300-acre working farm and game preserve in Chestertown, Maryland, called Remington Farms. On January 3 and 4, 1972, Remington hosted three FBI officials at Remington Farms and paid for their room, board, hunting licenses and stamps at a cost of $203.50. Twelve other FBI officials were hosted at the Remington Farm on three subsequent occasions, costing the arms dealer an additional $1,168 in room and board.

Remington also paid for liquor, ammunition, guides and game shot on these four weekends. Although a breakdown by individual is not available for these costs, Remington spent a total of $2,013.96 for forty seven individuals for the four weekends. Fifteen of the forty seven guests were then active FBI officials.

FBI records show that the Remington Firearms Company has not been awarded a firearms contract since 1971. The hunting weekends mentioned above all occurred after 1971. Six ammunition (not firearms) contracts have been awarded to Remington since fiscal year 1971, but each of these contracts was solicited and awarded after open bidding by the Justice Department. Although several of the FBI officials who attended the hunting weekends were in a position to influence the awarding of arms contracts, no arms contracts were awarded to Remington during the 1970's. Nor were arms contracts awarded during this time to Winchester Firearms Company which hosted a hunting weekend for three Bureau officials in 1973.

The Federal illegal gratuities statute, Title 18, United States Code, Sections 201 (f) and (g), requires that the gratuity shall be "for or because of" an official act.

This investigation found no evidence that the recipients of the gratuities did anything for Remington or Winchester, and therefore, there was no evidence warranting prosecution under this statute. The evidence does indicate that the Departmental regulation prohibiting the accepting of gifts or entertainment from those having or seeking a contractual relationship with the United States was violated. 28 C.F.R. §45.735-14(a). Moreover, the evidence shows that these employees also violated the general Departmental prohibition against conduct creating the appearance of impropriety. 28 C.F.R. §45.735-2. The Attorney General has referred this matter to the FBI Director with instructions to take appropriate administrative action against these employees.

J. Miscellaneous Allegations

1. Financial Dealings Between Joseph C. Palumbo and John P. Mohr

This investigation received information from the House Select Committee on Intelligence that John P. Mohr and Joseph C. Palumbo of Charlottesville, Virginia had had improper financial dealings. Mr. Palumbo and Mr. Mohr entered a financial arrangement in late 1972, after Mr. Mohr had retired from the FBI. The transaction was entirely lawful and at arms length and no evidence was found that Mr. Palumbo ever discussed the FBI or its activities with Mr. Mohr.

2. Official and Confidential Files

During 1975, an investigation was conducted into the disposition of the "official and confidential files" of J. Edgar Hoover following his death in May 1972. The inquiry determined that the files were turned over to Assistant Director W. Mark Felt by Miss Helen W. Gandy, Executive Assistant to Mr. Hoover, on May 4, 1972, and now are located at FBI headquarters. No evidence was found that official FBI files of any kind were removed to Mr. Hoover's home following his death.

A. PART II Summary and Actions Taken Against Principal Subjects

1. John P. Mohr

(a) Mr. Mohr was Assistant Director for the Administrative Division of the FBI and the Assistant to the Director. He was primarily responsible for using USRC as an exclusive supplier of electronics equipment to the FBI. His conduct toward§, USRC violated 28 C.F.R. 045.735-2(b) and (c)(2) (prohibiting employees from giving preferential treatment to any person outside the Department). He received a few gratuities (tape deck, Christmas gifts) from Mr. Tait. No evidence was found that he was bribed, but he violated 945.73514(a)(1), which prohibits employees from accepting gifts from those doing business with the Department. (b) FBI employees provided goods and services to him as described above. This arguably violated 18 U.S.C. 641 (conversion of government property to his own use), (prosecution barred by the statute of limitations), and 28 C.F.R.

§45.73516 (misuse of federal property). (c) Mr. Mohr was also responsible, along with Mr. Callahan, for using FBI Recreation Association and Confidential Fund monies for unauthorized public relations purposes. This matter has been referred to the Department's office of Management and Finance for appropriate action (see footnote 12 above). In 1972, he attended an expense paid hunting weekend at Remington Farms, an FBI arms supplier. This is a violation of the Department prohibition against accepting gifts from those doing business with the Department, 28 C.F.R. §45.735-14(a)(1). (d) No action has been taken against Mr. Mohr. He retired on June 30, 1972. Criminal action under all of the above federal provisions is barred by the five year statute of limitations.

2. Nicholas P. Callahan

Mr. Callahan was Assistant Director for the FBI's Administrative Division and later Associate Director. In 1976, pursuant to Attorney General Levi's order, he was asked to resign as a result of this investigation. He did resign.

(a) Mr. Callahan was responsible for improperly diverting thousands of dollars of FBIRA and Confidential Fund monies to official FBI public relations activities. The funds were not authorized or appropriated for public relations activities. There was no evidence that he converted these funds to his personal use, and therefore, no evidence warranting prosecution. This matter has been referred to the Department's Office of Management and Finance for appropriate action. (See footnote 12 above.)

(b) Mr. Callahan admitted receiving FBI goods and services. FBI employees decorated his beach house, built a fence, walnut shelves, and other furniture for his residence. The statute of limitations bars prosecution of Mr. Callahan for receiving government property in violation of 18 U.S.C.641.

(c) No evidence was found that Mr. Callahan was bribed or that he received illegal gratuities.

(d) No further action has been taken against Mr. Callahan.

3. Ivan W. Conrad

Mr. Conrad was employed by the FBI Laboratory in many positions from 1934 to 1973. He retired on July 12, 1973, as Assistant Director of the Laboratory.

   (a) Mr. Conrad took many pieces of electronic recording and amplifying equipment home with him and used them for his own benefit. Mr. Conrad asserted he had the equipment for legitimate purposes. The Department recovered all equipment, and Mr. Conrad tendered a $1,500 cashier's check to pay for his use of the equipment.
   (b) No further action has been taken against Mr. Conrad. Prosecution was barred, in the judgement of the Criminal Division, by the statute of limitations and because of the lack of evidence showing criminal intent on the part of Mr. Conrad.

4. Clarence M. Kelley

Director Kelley received the limited amount of goods and services described above. He was not involved in any of the other matters which are the subject of this report. Attorney General Levi and Deputy Attorney General Tyler determined that no disciplinary action was called for, but that Director Kelley should reimburse the Bureau for the goods and services he received. That has been done and no further action against him has been taken. Director Kelley should be given credit for putting an end to the improper practices described in the report. His cooperation greatly assisted Departmental investigators in uncovering the facts. His cooperation made this report possible. It should also be noted that Director Kelley was primarily responsible for bringing about the internal reforms set forth in the final section of this report.

5. G. Speights McMichael

Mr. McMichael is no longer in charge of, but continues to work in, the FBI's Property Procurement and Management Section. He is no longer cashier of the Imprest Fund, a petty cash reimbursement fund.

(a) Mr. McMichael clearly neglected his responsibilities in managing the Imprest Fund. There is some evidence that he permitted violations of

(b) procedures to favor USRC in the purchase of electronic equipment. 41 U.S.C. 252(c)(12). There is no evidence of bribery.

(c) While serving as the FBI's chief procurement officer, he attended an expense paid hunting weekend at Remington Farms. This is a probable violation of the Department regulation prohibiting the receipt of gifts from those doing business with the Department. 28 C.F.R. §45.735 14 (a) (1).

(d) The evidence that Mr. McMichael knowingly approved Imprest Fund reimbursement for the personal purchases of an FBI employee is not substantial. There is no evidence that he converted government money to his own use. 18 U.S.C. 641 and 643.

(e) McMichael clearly failed to meet his responsibilities as the FBI's Chief Procurement officer and probably violated 28 C.F.R. 945.73513 (misuse of official position) and 945.735-16 (misuse of federal property). His attendance at Remington Farms probably violated §45.735-14 (gifts from Department contractors). He failed to assist Department investigators. The statute of limitations bars criminal action against Mr. McMichael. These matters have, however, been referred to the Director with instructions to institute appropriate administrative action against him.

6. Joseph X. Tait

(a) On June 20, 1977, a jury acquitted Mr. Tait of. charges that he understated his income in 1971, 1972 and 1973, in violation of 26 U.S.C. 7201.
(b) A jury acquitted Mr. Tait on all counts of charges that he violated 18 U.S.C. 287 (false claims on the United States), 371 (conspiracy to defraud), and 1341 (mail fraud).
(c) Further comment regarding Mr. Tait is considered inappropriate because, unlike the other subjects of this report, he is not a government official.

B. Possible Civil Actions

1. U.S. Recording Company

The Department is considering taking civil action to invalidate USRC contracts and recover the excess profits obtained from the Bureau. The basis of such a suit would be the clear breach of applicable government procurement regulations. The Civil Division is now evaluating the relevant facts to determine whether the Department should institute a civil recovery action against the United States Recording Company or its president.

2. Conversion of Government Property by Bureau Officials

Civil actions may not be instituted because: the actual amounts involved are small compared to the expense of litigation; there would be substantial difficulty in fixing the government's loss with any appreciable accuracy; and, much of the government's property has already been returned. In addition, civil action may be barred by the statute of limitations.

3. Imprest Fund

Approximately, $1,700 was diverted from that fund for clearly improper purposes.

The property obtained with Imprest Fund monies has been returned to the Bureau. This matter has been referred to the Department's Office of Management and Finance to review the facts, and to take necessary administrative action.

4. Confidential Fund

Approximately, $75,000 was spent to purchase electronic equipment and $23,000 was spent over a fifteen year period on public relations type matter. This matter has also been referred to the Department's Office of Management and Finance for appropriate administrative action.

5. FBI Recreation Association

Monies from the FBI Recreation Association were improperly diverted. According to the Civil Division, the Government lacks standing to initiate any civil action, except under a somewhat strained theory of parens patriae. Accordingly, no civil action will be instituted regarding this matter.

C. Action Taken to Prevent Recurrence

Within the last fifteen months, Director Kelley has taken the following corrective measures to prevent the recurrence of the improper practices described in this report.He has:

1. Reorganized the Inspection Division and renamed it the Planning And Inspection Division; created the office of Professional Responsibility, an office of

Inspections, and an office of Planning and Evaluation;' established within the office of Inspections a separate Audit Unit, responsible for auditing all FBI funds and financial transactions; and organized the Division so that it reports directly to him, as Director.

2. Removed the Property Procurement and Management Section from the Division with budget responsibility, the Finance and Personnel Division, thereby making one Division head responsible for procurement and another responsible for the FBI budget and funds. Director Kelley has placed a Special Agent Accountant, a Certified Public Accountant, as Section Chief of the Property Procurement and Management Section.

3. Discontinued the use of the U.S. Recording Company as a "cover" or "cutout" for confidential purposes and established controls to ensure that all purchases are made in accordance with government regulations.

4. Restructured the FBI inventory system, to provide built-in controls and audit trails, and initiated automation of the inventory system to provide better accountability.

5. Discontinued the FBI Laboratory and Exhibits Sections' practice of providing personal services to FBI officials. Director Kelley also has discontinued the use of the unauthorized cash fund once maintained in the Exhibits Section.

6. Reorganized the management and handling of the FBI Recreation Association (FBIRA) and its funds, so that FBIRA officers are aware of their responsibilities to prevent unauthorized expenditures. A new treasurer of the FBIRA has taken office and is not responsible for any other FBI fund.

7. Replaced the FBI Confidential Fund with the Field Support Account, an imprest fund approved

by the Treasury Department and administered in accordance with Treasury and Justice Department regulations.

8. Developed and improved the FBI career development program for Special Agents to ensure that the best qualified individuals are selected for administrative advancement, substantially reducing the possibility that one person or group can control the selection of such candidates. In addition to these administrative measures, the FBI has increased legal instruction within its training curriculum; held training sessions on the FBI guidelines for career agents; and issued detailed instructions to the field on legal questions concerning the legality and propriety of investigative techniques. TheFBI is also posing such questions to the Department's Office of Legal Counsel with increasing frequency.

On January 3, 1978, the Attorney General referred the entire U.S. Recording Company matter to the FBI and instructed the Director to initiate administrative proceedings against G. Speights McMichael and other FBI employees whom the Director considers to be appropriate, subjects for administrative action. The Attorney General requested the Director to keep him advised by informing the Department's Counsel on Professional Responsibility of all administrative action taken.

Finally, the Attorney General has asked Director Kelley to bring to the Attorney General's attention any improper attempts to have FBI agents conduct investigations or undertake activities which are not within the Bureau's authorized jurisdiction. The Attorney General has also directed all Bureau personnel to bring reports of misconduct to the attention of appropriate Bureau officials, and when necessary, the office of Professional

Responsibility at the Bureau and at the Department of Justice.

_1/ 41 U.S.C. 252 (c) and regulations promulgated thereunder.

_2/ 41 U.S.C. 252 (c) (12).

_3/ The limit was raised to $10,000 by statutory amendment in 1974.

_4/ The Blue Ridge Club burned down on November 23, 1975, just before House Select Committee investigators were scheduled to interview Club employees. This investigation revealed that an eight-year-old child caused the fire while playing with matches. The child "confessed" to Department investigators. The testimony of other witnesses corroborates the confession.

_5/ A search of the transcripts of committee hearings revealed no evidence that Mr. Tait actually testified before the referenced subcommittee or any other subcommittee.

_6/ 28 C.F.R. §45.735-2(b) and (c) prohibit the giving of favored treatment or advantage to any member of the public and any action which might result in, or create the appearance of: preferential treatment, the use of public office for private gain, or an adverse effect on public confidence in the integrity of the Government. 28 C.F.R. X45.735-14(a)(1) prohibits the acceptance by public officials of gifts or gratuities from those doing business with the Department of Justice.

_7/ No official documents, memoranda, or work orders were found which account for the work performed, the materials used, or the goods produced by Exhibits Section employees for the personal benefit of Bureau officials.

_8/ Contrary to the evidence obtained from Exhibits Section employees, Mr. Callahan stated that he paid for the material for the fences and installed them himself on personal time.

_9/ Mr. Callahan testified that agents are allowed to take home cameras for personal use to maintain their proficiency with them. Agents assigned to this investigation verified that this is the case, but indicated that the practice is intended to maintain familiarity with cameras more complex than the Polaroid.

_10/ A further term of the agreement was that he make restitution for the goods he received in an amount to be determined later between his attorney and attorneys for the United States. On September 28, 1976, Dunphy was fined $500 and placed on probation. He returned all government materials to the Bureau, in accordance with the plea agreement.

There was no footnote _11/

_12/ Title 31 U.S.C. 628, a noncriminal statute, prohibits the use of appropriated funds for a purpose not specified in the appropriation. The Counsel on Professional Responsibility has requested the Department's Office of Management and Finance to review these facts, to take necessary administrative action to prevent the recurrence of this conduct, and if appropriate, to refer the matter to the Comptroller General for possible recovery actions against responsible disbursing officers.

DOJ-1978-M

The U S Recording fiasco was not the *only* "tomfoolery" going on within the FBI. I strongly urge all of you to obtain a copy of *Inside Hoover's FBI* by Neil J. Welch (one of Hoover's number two men). It has been out of print for a while but you may find a copy on Amazon or via one of the web search engines.

CHAPTER TEN

Bugging the FBI

In mid-1978, an executive vice president (EVP) of Northwestern Bank requested a visit to my facility. I had never dealt with this particular person but knew Duncan was involved with other more pressing matters. The EVP told me that the FBI had replaced the IRS as Duncan's chief antagonist and the FBI was totally disrupting the functioning and operations of Northwestern Bank. The FBI was using the old "divide and conquer" routine to demoralize and frighten the employees. The FBI started with lower-level employees and was working upward toward management. Duncan felt it would be a good idea if every manager carried a pocket recorder to recorded any and all conversations with the investigating agents. The language of his intent was clearly within the confines of the law, i.e., one-party consent. He also purchased three one-third speed cassette recorders to record conference room confrontations. The EVP left my facility with one of the one-third speed recorders and I ordered the remaining two for him.

Several weeks later, the EVP telephoned and indicated that there was one scenario they weren't prepared for: the making of recordings in a Northwestern Bank office controlled by the FBI. I told the EVP that regardless of the surroundings, the same one-party consent rule would apply.

A few days later, a Northwestern aircraft arrived at BWI airport to ferry me to North Wilkesboro. I was taken to the main bank building and shown the office the bank wanted to monitor. It was near a corner of the building that had glass windows all around. There was a roughly thirty-foot by thirty-foot open area in the corner that contained no furniture whatsoever. To the left was an office with the door open. Just outside the office were several knocked down cardboard boxes and tubes from vacuum cleaners. The inside of the office was absolutely sterile, with one desk, one chair, and one telephone (sitting the floor). As usual, I had brought some countermeasure equipment with me to do a quick check of any new and unfamiliar surroundings. I felt, after seeing the room, that it most likely was bugged and under video surveillance, so I set the countermeasure equipment aside. A quick glance out the window revealed an automobile pointing directly at me in the parking lot across the street. The EVP showed me the proposed listening post and I could see that the length of the run would need a preamplifier at the microphone end of the system.

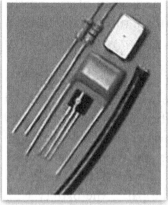

By then, I had serious reservations about the EVP. When he met me at the airport, he asked what I knew about citizen band antennas. He said the antennas he was using were melting at the base. When he opened the trunk of his car, I saw a 250-watt linear amplifier connected to his CB radio and the antennas simply couldn't handle that much power. No wonder the antennas were melting. The maximum legal amount of power for citizen band transmitters is 5 watts. When we reached his house, he offered me a mason jar full of moonshine. I allowed him to place it on the palm of my hand and then handed it back. On a table in the kitchen, he had another CB transmitter. This one had a 1,000-watt amplifier connected to it. The antenna outside boosted the signal by ten times so effectively, he was transmitting 10,000 watts. Most commercial radio stations do not transmit with that much power. He offered me the microphone but I declined it. I thought about contacting the FCC, but I already had too many battles going on. He gave me the keys to a pickup truck parked outside and I drove to the motel.

Based on the EVP's earlier description, I had taken only a microphone and hank of RG-174 coaxial cable.

Back at the motel, I pulled a couple of resistors, a capacitor, and a 2N3391A transistor out of one of my 1059 countermeasure preamps and constructed a microphone preamplifier. On my way back to the bank building, I stopped by the car I had seen earlier. The car had no tires and was sitting on four cinderblocks. It was covered with dust and debris and obviously had been sitting somewhere for a long time, but not there. There was no drip line around the car. Out came my contact microphone and when placed on the car, I heard the unmistakable sound of a time-lapse camera. I thought, and probably said out loud, *C'mon you guys, you can do better than this!*

On returning to the target room, I installed the microphone and preamp inside the telephone jack cover. At the access point nearest Bower's office, I connected my 1059 preamplifier and threw on the J4 power switch. I turned up the volume and could clearly hear the sound of an empty room. A sense of pride came over me. I was satisfied I had earned my money. I gave Bower the parts, the battery with connector, and a schematic and drawing he would need to connect to the target wires in his telephone. I was convinced he lacked the technical expertise to follow my instructions and I was right. I packed my bags and left town on one of Northwestern's airplanes.

A few days after my return to Cockeysville, I received a call from Bower saying, "We can't hear a thing!" I was ready for that remark. *Yeah!*

Shortly afterward, Duncan was indicted for misapplication of several hundred thousand dollars of the bank's money. He was convicted of misapplying $675.00. Thanks to one of the idiotsyncrasies of our legal system, the sentencing guidelines are based on what you are *charged* with, not what you are *convicted* of, and Duncan was given a three-year sentence. He was now a broken man. The vultures came to feed, and feed they did.

To thank him for all he had done for them, 1,500 people came to Duncan's sendoff party. Do you have that many friends? Duncan was a giant of a man in North Carolina and a super patriot to boot. He had helped thousands of people during his term as Chairman of Northwestern Bank. Now, that was all to end.

Shortly afterward, Duncan, Starr, and the EVP were charged with bugging the FBI. They had extremely bad counsel. Rather than stick with their lawful position of one-party consent, counsel came up with all kinds of rinky-dink defenses and got them all convicted. What Duncan and others didn't know, and I would later discover, was the FBI had absolutely no evidence whatsoever that the device I installed was ever used. To counter that problem, one of the FBI agents, using one of the tape recorders seized from Northwestern Bank, fabricated a tape recording of an alleged telephone call. It was then used in evidence in Duncan's trial and I am sure it led to his conviction.

Later, I would have the opportunity to actually listen to that recording the FBI used to indict Duncan and it was indeed a fabrication. Over my many years of association with the intelligence community, I have listened to hundreds of intelligence recordings. They *all* have the same information: empty or silent room noise. It *is* there and cannot be removed. If you want to hear it, take a tape recorder, put it on a desktop or whatever, turn it on record, and leave the room for fifteen minutes. Return, listen to the recording, and you will hear exactly what I mean, The Smithsonian Institution and Futurism/Johns Hopkins University recently published research papers claimig that "Silence has a sound" that support exactly what I am saying. Smithsonian Institution: https://apple.news/ A8JTt1tUZRBKVPOV7S9czBQ FUTURISM/JHU: https://apple.news/ AenvL3wR8QNacZkL-bKMMBQ

The Criminal Case

In early December 1978, I was subpoenaed to appear before the grand jury that had indicted Duncan, Starr, and the EVP. My attorney, Bud Fensterwald, paralegal Marc Feldman, and I headed to North Carolina. Before leaving, Bud told me to type up two three by five cards with the Fifth Amendment statement on them (for you foreigners, the fifth amendment of the US Constitution gives a citizen the right *not* to answer a question). Before going into the grand jury room, Fensterwald instructed me to give them my name, rank, and serial number and then "read the card." I must have read the first card sixty to seventy times before I ceremoniously set it aside, pulled out the second card, and started reading it. Of course, it had on it the exact same statement. One of the grand jurors joked that the first card must have run out of gas. In total, I must have taken the fifth 150 to 175 times.

Periodically, whenever I got tired, I excused myself to converse with my attorney (i.e., get a breather). When I reentered the room, Fensterwald would say, "Read the card."

Immediately after I was dismissed from the grand jury, Marc Feldman grabbed me by the arm and took me to an empty room. He asked me to tell him *exactly* what I had seen in the grand jury room. I started to my immediate right with the U.S.'s attorney, then the stenographer, then the grand jurors, describing them one by one. Finally, I described the jury foreman's table at which sat two men. One was a gray-haired fellow and the other FBI Agent XB. Feldman gasped and told me to go over that part again, which I did. A couple of days later, I received a copy of a motion from Fensterwald to the court asking that the charges be dropped due to improprieties by the FBI. This was a serious issue. It is a violation of federal law for an investigating agent to be present when a witness is questioned.

The court requested a hearing. It stood to reason that I would take the stand, say he was there, and say that he, knowing he had violated federal law and been caught, would most certainly say he was not. The only way to

ON ADVICE OF CONSEL, I RESPECTFULLY DECLINE ANSWERING THAT QUESTION ON THE GROUNDS THAT IT MAY TEND TO IN-CRIMINATE ME.

solve that dilemma was to put a couple of grand jurors on the stand under oath and ask what they saw. To help me decide which of the grand jurors we would use the court was forced to give me a list of the names and addresses of the grand jurors—and here are twenty-one of them.
You will read more about these people later.

Bernice C Poole
Bx 8694 2159
Charles St Durham,
NC 27707

Carl F. Spaugh, Jr.
2441 W
Clemmonsville
Winston-Salem, NC
27107

Jarius J. Watson
General Delivery
Efland, NC 27243

Hilda J Weaver
1008 Twyckenham
Dr Greensville, NC
27408

Dorothy R
McDougald
Box 471
Broadway, NC
27505

Richard K Burr
2852 Wyclif Road
Raleigh, NC 27602
Foreman

Rebecca A Myers
1530 Harding St
Winston-Salem, NC
27107
Deputy Foreman

Mable L Parker
39 Walnut Street
Concord, NC 28025

Lucy J Pearson
3707 Prospect Dr
Winston-Salem, NC
27107

Leeoist B Kime Rt 2
Box 38 Liberty, NC
27298

Doris A King
Rt 3 Box 385A
Lexington, NC
27289

John W Leonard
4502 Summit Ave
Greensboro, NC
27405

David C Campbell
4 Crestvies Cir
Salisbury, NC 28144

Johnny S Mason
2706 Ferrell Road
Durham, NC 27704

Billy Hegwood
4955 Shattalon Dr
Winston-Salem, NC
27106

Evelyn P Furr
Route 3
Albemarle, NC
28001

Edith J Johnson
1617 E 23 St
Winston-Salem, NC
27105

Patricia Kennedy
Rt 4 Box 1179
Winston-Salem, NC
27105

Carl H Brown
Rt 2 Box153
Trinity, NC 27370

Raney W Fourshee
1055 Chatfield Dr
Greensboro, NC
27410

Jarius J Watson
General Dellivery
Efland, NC 27243

Jackson
No Further
Information

I had transferred these names from my master list to four names and addresses per mailing label group. I have since misplaced my master list and one group of three names and addresses. As soon as I find either, those names will be added to the above list.

So Much for Grand
Jury Secrecy!

I took the stand and, under oath, made my statement that the FBI agent was indeed there. The FBI agent said he was not. Even though I took the oath to tell the truth, the whole truth, and nothing but the truth, no oath was given to him. He should have stopped right there but his ego simply would not let him. The FBI agent, not the court, asked Fensterwald if he had seen him go in and out of the grand jury room. Fensterwald's answer was, "No." Again, the FBI agent couldn't shut up. He commented that he was in the library while I was before the grand jury.

The judge should have immediately responded, "Hey, wait a second. You know as well as I that directly behind the jury foreman's desk is a door that opens into a covered corridor that ends at the library! Maybe we *should* hear from some of those grand jurors!" Instead, the judge turned to me and said, "Mr. Kaiser, you're mistaken, honest or otherwise." Whack went the gavel and that was that. At least my team now knew what kind of trash we were up against. My team later learned that the two FBI agents had previously appeared before another grand jury who refused to indict me as well as a magistrate who refused to indict me. This was their third try and they had to do it in a dirty, filthy, underhanded way.

Once back in Washington, Fensterwald received notice of the arraignment date. On that date, my team packed up our briefs and belongings and headed back to North Carolina. The US attorney sent word that he wanted to see us in his office. When we arrived, he was sitting behind his desk. We chatted with him briefly about nothings. Shortly, FBI Agent XB entered the office. The US attorney got up from his desk and joined us at the front of the desk. The FBI agent then took the seat behind the desk and now *he* became the prosecuting attorney. He indicated that we surely had sufficient time to study the indictment and that the only logical response was a guilty plea. *Wrong!* I said *nothing*, but Fensterwald thanked him and we left.

Had the agent made even a cursory review of my FBI file, he would have known what an idiotic suggestion it was. If I had entered a guilty plea, I would have lost any security clearances I had at the time. I would have lost my charter membership in the International Association of Bomb Technicians (IABTI). I would have lost my passport and ability to travel freely. I would have lost my "plank" (a Navy honor started in the 1700s) at the Navy Explosive Ordnance School in Indian Head, Maryland, where I had taught on a regular basis for over ten years. I would have lost my amateur radio license that I had held for twenty-five years, and I would have lost my dignity and self-respect. The FBI agent wasn't the only one who wanted to throw me in the slammer. My wife suggested I plead guilty to the lesser charge, spend a couple of years in prison, and then they'd forget about me. *Sure!*

When we appeared for arraignment, there were twenty-three cases on the docket, including mine. As expected, I was last on the list. Twenty-two of the defendants, all men, had *no* counsel present. My team and I stood at the rear of the courtroom. I can't begin to express my emotions when all twenty-two of the other defendants, *without counsel*, entered a plea of guilty. There was no doubt in my mind that they were all FBI agents. Something about what was going on was way more than "fishy." Fensterwald winked at me. From experience, he knew that on numerous occasions when people were not represented by council, the court would watch the defendant they wanted to screw. They would wait until he or she went to the bathroom or whatever. He also knew that sometimes the court docket was stuffed with FBI agents whose primary use was to waste time and intimidate the defendant. The court would then immediately shift the defendant's position on the docket. When the defendant did not immediately appear when called, the court would cite him or her for *contempt of court*. Obviously, I was covered. My punishment was that my "legal money meter" at $400.00 per hour (in 1978 dollars) kept running for an entire day. Once my not guilty plea was entered, we headed back to Washington. I did, however, have to leave my passport behind. The FBI must have convinced the court that I was a "flight risk." What they didn't realize was they had taken on a "fight risk."

Back in Washington, Fensterwald turned me over to the FBI for my "official" arrest. The FBI tried to extract new information from me to no avail. One of the agents made a technical error that I felt duty bound to correct since it could be a major issue later on. He asked about the 15/32 inch per second recorders I had sold Northwestern Bank. I told him they were 15/16 inch per second recorders similar to the ones I had sold the FBI in the past. I was fingerprinted and a palm print was taken. The jar of moonshine came to mind. I was then put in handcuffs, taken to the bowels of the DC jail, and locked in a cell. An apple was my only company. Fensterwald was busy upstairs before a judge trying to arrange bail for me. I sat in the cell a looong time. Then, I was summoned before a woman judge who reviewed the case and wondered why I was there in the first place. She released me on my personal recognizance without bail. Back to the cell I went. When my release order reached the jailer, he looked at it and, with the eraser on his pencil, pushed it to the far corner of his desk. Occasionally, he would pull it toward himself, again using the eraser on his pencil, and then push it back. Finally, without a word, he unlocked the cell and pointed to the stairway.

One day, I mentioned to my friend Capt. Jim Regan (now deceased) of the Pennsylvania State Police that the FBI had handcuffed me with my palms apart.

He told me it was an old intimidation trick used to intimidate "hardened criminals." Didn't work.

Next came the task of choosing a jury pool. Fensterwald felt at least 250 people would have to be interviewed in order to find the required number of jurors and alternates. My team (including me) and the US attorney met in the judge's chamber. The FBI agent knew enough by now *not* to be there. One by one, the potential jurors were asked by the judge, "Do you have any predisposition as to the guilt or innocence of Mr. Kaiser?"

Well over 200 said, "Based on the pretrial publicity in this case, I would have to find him guilty." Obviously, that process took a big chunk of very expensive time, but finally we had our twelve jurors and a few alternates.

The trial date was now approaching and there was a lot of preparatory work to do. My job was to contact the character witnesses my team had chosen and give them an approximate appearance date. My law enforcement friends would have to be subpoenaed because that was the only way I could get them out of their offices.

The lawyers spent the first couple of days sparring with the US attorney. At the right table were the US attorney and FBI Agent XB. At the left table was my team. Finally, the US attorney brought on their FBI "technical expert" to describe how he found my microphone and amplifier. He tried his damndest to make it sound like a sophisticated device but he wasn't very convincing. He told the jury that the device used "crossed pairs" of telephone wires, a technique used only by the best of eavesdroppers. I blushed and was deeply humbled. I thought to myself, *The FBI thinks I'm the best of eavesdroppers! Wow!* In telephone company lingo, a pair is a wire with identical background color and a stripe on it of the same color, e.g., yellow-red and red-yellow. I actually never gave it a thought. The closet where the wires started was dark and I grabbed the brightest wires of the bunch: yellow. I then searched through the yellow wires until I found the standard single line telephone colors: red and green. That

121

meant I used yellow-red and yellow-green—a single wire from two pairs. So what if the light was bad? Crossed pairs... phooey!

After nearly an entire day, the FBI expert finally finished. Now it was our turn to cross-examine him. In what I viewed as the greatest courtroom theatrics I had ever seen, Fensterwald slowly rose, adjusted and buttoned his jacket, adjusted the collar on his jacket, and made sure his sleeves were the same length. He said, "Agent XT, you have been very kind in describing to the jury how you found the device. Would you please tell the jury where you got the equipment to do your job?"

Agent XT pointed at me and responded, "From the defendant over there—Marty, I guess."

At that point, I realized that Fensterwald had *really blown it*! He never asked Agent XT if he had tested the microphone to see if it really worked. Fensterwald thanked him, said, "No further questions, your honor," and ceremoniously sat down. You can imagine the headlines the next day: "FBI Uses Kaiser Equipment to Find Kaiser Bug."

Well...

After the FBI technical agent finished, the prosecution put on the stand a variety of witnesses that included just about everybody with the bank who had touched my invoice. When they were asked how they knew it was an invoice, most responded, "Experience." My invoice was one of those fold-up kind, where one-half inch of each side is folded in first and then the rest is folded into thirds. One of the witnesses revealed the amount of the invoice could be easily seen, even though it had never been opened. He told the court you could squeeze the top and bottom of the envelope, which would then open it enough so you could read what was inside. To this day, that invoice has never been paid. In any event, Fensterwald pried a lot of valuable information out of the prosecution's witnesses.

Unfortunately, no one mentioned how ridiculous it would be for someone to invoice for a criminal act.

Now it was my turn to take the stand. I had with me all of the equipment and parts I had originally taken to Northwestern bank. I talked through and did what I did to build the device. Although my hands shook a bit, I got it built. The entire time I was giving my testimony, I was deathly afraid the issue of the fabricated tape would come up. If it had, it would have placed my wife, children, and myself in grave danger and destroy my business. All of my testimony skillfully avoided falling into that trap. The device I had just built was then given to the prosecution and the FBI tech expert. As I left the stand, I started to walk toward the prosecution table but Fensterwald shook his head *no* and I never went anywhere near it.

He put my secretary on the stand. She told of my day-to-day operations and that there was no secrecy involved when she typed the invoice for Northwestern.

Next, we put on a vice president from Knowles Electronics, the manufacturer of the microphone. This person told the court that Knowles ships tens of thousands of their microphones each year and that none are "primarily designed for the interception of oral communications," a key component of one of the charges against me. I later learned from Dr. Knowles's biography that he was concerned the FBI might restrict sales of his products. That fact was described in his biography *Now Hear This: The Life of Hugh S. Knowles, Acoustical Engineer and Entrepreneur.*

Perhaps the most notorious case of an "other" use of KE equipment was that of Martin Kaiser, dubbed by some the "Michelangelo of Electronics" because of his uncanny ability to create a listening gadget with juiced-up wires and just about anything. Whenever he could, Kaiser used only Knowles equipment because he thought it was "simply the best for the bugging business."

During the 1960s and1970s, he did up to $200,000 worth of such business annually with government intelligence agencies. For many years Kaiser's remarkable and tiny surveillance devices were especially sought after by the FBI, but then, in what he called the "swamp of the post-Hoover FBI" Kaiser's relationship with the government gumshoes went awry. As reported by Newsweek in December 1975 Kaiser went before congress to testify that FBI agents were buying his equipment and then cooking the books to show "U.S. Recording" as the supplier, with a hefty markup. Kaiser was respected for his uncompromising honesty, and by the time his charges had been fully investigated (according to a later Justice Department report) the General Accounting Office found that agents had indeed routed $24 million through U.S. Recording and did indeed personally pocketing some $7.5 million of it. Even before the GAO's findings were reported, however, Kaiser ceased doing business with the FBI. In 1977 Kaiser was indicted in Winston-Salem, North Carolina on trumped-up charges that he had bugged the FBI and illegally transported electronic equipment across state lines. In fact, Kaiser had been hired by a bank in North Wilkesboro, NC simply to bug an office. Later, when FBI agents investigated the bank and used the office that Kaiser had allegedly bugged, they seized the opportunity to file charges against him. Before proceedings in the trial of the United States of America vs Martin L. Kaiser began in February 1978, Kaiser filed a pre-trial affidavit that the FBI was seeking revenge against him.

Among the several expert witnesses called upon to testify on behalf of the defendant during the trial was Knowles Electronics marketing manager Harry F. Waller Jr. Waller confirmed that Kaiser was a long-standing customer and user of Knowles products. He also verified that all but two of the subminiature microphones brought into evidence were standard Knowles products used mostly, but not exclusively, in hearing aids. Waller cited the various other applications— in headsets for telephone operators and pilots, walkie-talkies for policemen and firemen, acoustic monitoring for medical purposes, and bomb detection—of the exhibited microphone models, several hundred thousand of each of which Knowles produced annually. Fearful that a verdict might be rendered that would somehow inhibit the sale of his products across state lines, Hugh instructed his legal counsel to stay on top of the case. But after just one week of proceedings, the jury found Kaiser not guilty, and the nasty affair had no lasting effect on Knowles sales or reputation.[3]

Next came time for my character witnesses. With the exception of a few non-law enforcement witnesses all of my law enforcement witness had not arrived. I called a few only to learn that they had not received their subpoenas and could not come until they did. A subpoena is a normal requirement in law enforcement circles.

Fensterwald rushed to the clerk's office only to learn that the clerk had "forgotten" to send them out. *Suuure!* The clerk of the court would prove to be the biggest *scumbag* I have ever known. That kept the money meter running for a couple of days until all witnesses were in the courtroom.

Here is a list of my character witnesses.

MSgt. Mike Lizak (now deceased), Army explosive ordnance disposal EOD, Holder of Bronze Star and Purple Heart
Capt. Gil Karner (now deceased), Baltimore City Bomb Squad
Capt. James Regan (now deceased), Pennsylvania State Police Intelligence
Capt. XX, US Capitol Police
Lt. Tom Plasay (now deceased), Baltimore County Homicide
Lt. Cliff Lund (now deceased), Baltimore County Bomb Squad
Cleve Clevland, electronic engineer

Al Montifusco, CIA

---

[3] Susan Goodwillie, *Now Hear This: The Life of Hugh S. Knowles, Acoustical Engineer and Entrepreneur* (London, UK: Francis Press, 1999), page.

The prosecuting attorney savagely attacked each character witness, demanding to know why he would associate with a slime ball like me. They accurately relayed their past experience with me, which was outstanding. I later spoke with Captain Regan about the disrespect the prosecuting attorney had shown. He told me it was part of the game and happens to him all the time.

That didn't make it right.

Just before we got to the CIA agent's turn, the doors of the courtroom crashed open and in rushed two men dressed in grey suits and pointy-toed shoes and carrying black attaché cases. Without saying a word and with a bang of the door, they marched straight into the judge's chambers. The judge whacked his gavel and said, "Chambers, gentlemen." With that Fensterwald, Feldman, the prosecuting attorney, *and* the FBI agent (the very agent who several months earlier asked for and received permission to sue me civilly after he was done beating me up in criminal court) went into the judge's chambers. I wasn't asked.

Hello out there! Does anyone see any problem with this?

Fensterwald told me that while in the room, each side had to prepare a list of twenty questions that would be taken to CIA headquarters by the guys with the pointy-toed shoes and personally approved by Director Stamfield Turner. A day went by before the guys with the pointy-toed shoes returned with a list of ten approved questions for each side. It was my turn first, so we put the CIA agent on the stand and asked him our ten questions. We got the ten prearranged answers we expected. The agent was then turned over to the prosecuting attorney who arose and began tearing up the list. The judge whacked his gavel and ordered all to return to his chamber.

When they came back, the prosecuting attorney said, "No further questions." Talk about arrogance!

The case eventually went to the jury and I was found not guilty. Fensterwald and I went into the hallway to stretch our legs just as the jury filed out of the jury room. They walked in single file with a look of terror and disbelief on their faces. They were equidistance apart, looking at the nape of the neck of the person in front. Fensterwald nudged me and said, "Thank them." As each passed by, I loudly said, "Thank you." *No one*, absolutely *no one*, turned to acknowledge my thanks. My friend, ex-CIA agent Marshall Soghoian, later confirmed what I suspected: the jury was not acting alone. Later, when Fensterwald and I were giving a statement to a reporter from the *Winston-Salem Journal*, FBI agent XB walked by. The reporter turned to him and asked what his plans were now that I had been found innocent. The FBI agent angrily responded, "Mr. Kaiser is *not* innocent. He was found not guilty only of the three charges brought against him."

Later, I made a statement to Fensterwald that I was glad of the outcome because it set precedent for others who would follow me. Fensterwald said, "Wrong!" He told me that the *only* way to set precedent is to be found *guilty* and then have the case overturned on appeal. So there you have it folks. Once the legal system entraps you, you can't get out without the legal system.

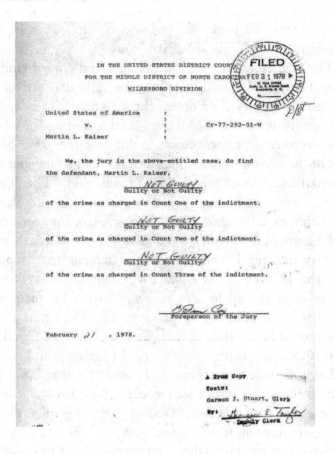

IN THE UNITED STATES DISTRICT COURT
FOR THE MIDDLE DISTRICT OF NORTH CAROLINA
WILKESBORO DIVISION

FILED
FEB 21 1978

United States of America :

    v.   :   Cr-77-292-01-W

Martin L. Kaiser   :

We, the jury in the above-entitled case, do find
the defendant, Martin L. Kaiser,

NOT GUILTY
Guilty or Not Guilty

of the crime as charged in Count One of the indictment.

NOT GUILTY
Guilty or Not Guilty

of the crime as charged in Count Two of the indictment.

NOT GUILTY
Guilty or Not Guilty

of the crime as charged in Count Three of the indictment.

Foreperson of the Jury

February 21, 1978.

A True Copy
Test:
Carson J. Stuart, Clerk
By:
Deputy Clerk

Winston-Salem Journal

Tuesday, February 21, 1978

Jury May Get Case Today, Is Kaiser Object of FBI Vendetta?

Twelve jurors probably will begin deliberations today to decide whether Martin L. Kaiser is guilty of conspiracy and illegally bugging FBI agents while they investigated Northwestern Bank last year.

One thing the jury must decide is whether the FBI is carrying out a vendetta against Kaiser, one of the country's foremost wiretap and bugging experts.

Kaiser, a manufacturer of surveillance devices from Maryland, was once a major supplier of the FBI's surveillance equipment But his dealings with the FBI stopped when he publicly identified an FBI front company used to buy his products and resell them to government agencies at substantially higher prices. Today, Kaiser no longer works with the FBI, but his clients include the CIA, the Army and Air Force, several foreign countries and more than 200 police departments.

Martin Kaiser is still one of the most respected makers of bugging equipment in the world—among his character references is the head of the CIA's procurement division. Kaiser still supplies the...with a great deal of surveillance gear' and he still holds an agency rating of secret.

But Kaiser says that the FBI wants revenge on him. He alleges that the FBI seeks revenge because of his testimony before the presidentially appointed National Wiretap Commission and the House Select Committee on Intelligence in 1975. In his testimony before the panels Kaiser revealed links between the FBI and U.S. Recording Co., an electronic equipment purchasing company.

Kaiser told the committee that the recording company was actually an FBI front—an apparently legitimate private business. Which was in fact operated by high ranking FBI officials. Kaiser had done a considerable amount of business with the FBI, he said, but his business began to suffer greatly after he was instructed in 1969 to sell his equipment to U.S. Recording instead of directly to the FBI.

Kaiser testified that he first assured that the procedure was merely a security measure,—but he later discovered that the electronic devices he sold to U.S. Recording were being duplicated and resold at substantial markups.

Kaiser had sold the FBI many surveillance devices—among them the bug detection kit used to find the listening devices Kaiser is charged with installing at Northwestern's headquarters in Wilkesboro. After his testimony an investigation by the General Accounting Office revealed that the FBI front company had marked up the prices of Kaiser's gear from 12 percent to 280 percent.

Kaiser testified that the FBI was not the only group buying his products through U.S. Recording. In addition to federal agencies, Kaiser told the congressional committee foreign governments, including Canada and Iran bought the marked-up goods.

Kaiser now says that most—of his federal contracts were severed after he brought the front company to public attention. An affidavit Kaiser filed in federal court claims that his sales to the various intelligent agencies plummeted from $200,000.00 annually before his testimony to $450 year afterward and then $000,000.00 for the rest of his companies existence.

His allegations of a vendetta go well beyond the U.S. Recording Co. payment scheme, though. Kaiser said that Thomas J. Brereton, the FBI agent in charge of the Northwestern investigation illegally attended grand jury proceedings while Kaiser was testifying.

Kaiser's allegations resulted in a special hearing called by Judge Hiram H. Ward in U.S. Middle District Court here last month. Ward ruled that Brereton had not improperly attended the grand jury hearings and that "a mistake had been made, honest or otherwise."

Brereton testified that he had been in the U.S. attorney's law library during Kaiser's grand jury appearance.

Friction between Kaiser and Brereton seemed to continue throughout the seven days of testimony in the bugging trial. Kaiser's attorneys repeatedly asked Ward to admonish Brereton for speaking with Assistant U.S. Attorney Benjamin White during cross examination.

Brereton consulted with White before many questions were put to defense witnesses, and Kaiser's attorneys objected that the jury could overhear Brereton's comments. Several times, Ward instructed Brereton to lower his voice when he spoke with the prosecutor.

A part of Kaiser's affidavit on the FBI vendetta matter said that two special FBI agents visited him in December 1975 to interview him on his U S. Recording Co. testimony. Kaiser said the two "literally held me for several hours hostage...to elicit a statement which repudiated my earlier congressional testimony and absolved the Bureau and U.S. Recording Co. of their wrongdoing."

The U.S. attorney's office filed a motion in federal court to deny Kaiser's allegations of a vendetta.

Kaiser's trial will continue at 9:30 a.m. today, with final arguments and instructions to the jury scheduled.

Winston-Salem Journal
Wednesday—February 22, 1978

Martin L. Kaiser has been found not guilty of bugging FBI agents, conspiracy and illegal transporting listening devices.

The verdict was returned by a jury of eight women and four men after 2.5 hours of deliberation yesterday afternoon in U.S. Federal District Court here.

Kaiser, an electronic surveillance expert from Cockeysville, MD, had been charged with helping Edwin Duncan Jr. and Gwen E. Bowers bug FBI agents who were investigating Northwestern Bank last year. Duncan, former bank board chairman, and Bowers, a former bank vice president, pleaded guilty to similar charges last November.

The bugging took place between April and July 1977 in an office in the bank's headquarters in Wilkesboro. "In all honesty," Kaiser said after the verdict was announced, "it's what we expected. Needless to say, I'm satisfied." Throughout the eight-day trial Kaiser admitted installing bugging equipment in a bank office used by the FBI agents but denied knowing that Duncan and Bowers would use the equipment illegally. The government case contended that Kaiser was fully aware that bank employees would use the bugging system to illegally monitor the FBI investigation.

"What this case is really about is human rights—the right to human privacy," said Assistant U.S. attorney Benjamin White in his final argument yesterday morning. "There is nothing illegal about him installing these devices—many attorneys have them in their offices, many businessmen have them in their offices," said John Morrow, one of Kaiser's attorneys.

Much of Kaiser's trial was marked by controversy over his past business dealings with the FBI. Kaiser, who is a major manufacturer of surveillance equipment for government agencies, filed a pretrial affidavit protesting that the FBI was seeking revenge against him.

Kaiser said the FBI wanted vengeance because of testimony he gave before congressional panels on surveillance matters. He had identified an FBI front company that bought his equipment and resold it to the FBI and other government agencies at marked-up prices.

Most of the defense witnesses were from law enforcement agencies, and most testified that Kaiser is reputable and trustworthy. Kaiser testified that at he sells bugging equipment and bomb detection gear to more than 200 law enforcement groups. His clients, he said, include the...the Army and Air Force and several foreign governments.

In his closing remarks, White questioned the nature of Kaiser's relations with his clients. After saying that Kaiser had once had the trust of law enforcement groups. White said, "Mr.

Kaiser sold that trust, ladies and gentlemen, for $3,500.00 (Kaiser's fee—for the Northwestern Bank bugging)."

Shortly after the end of the trial, one of Kaiser's attorneys told reporters that Northwestern has never paid Kaiser's fee. "We hope we don't have to sue them to get it—they're a big bank," said Bernard Fensterwald, a Washington lawyer who once defended James McCord, one of the Watergate burglars.

Kaiser said he plans to visit his daughter in Florida and then return to work. "I've really been out of business since July 29 (the date of his indictment)," he said. "I'm really looking forward to getting back to it."

Shortly after I returned to Cockeysville, Maryland, I sent the following letter to *all* of the grand jurors.

MARTIN L. KAISER, INC.
Countersurveillance · Bomb Detection · Surveillance Electronics

March 29, 1978
[Space for Grand Juror's address] Dear
[Grand Juror's name]:

Franklin Roosevelt said, "Events don't just happen, they're made to happen." Recently, you were part of an event that was made to happen.

Your name was provided to me by the Clerk of the Court in Greensboro as having been a member of the Grand Jury which returned a multi count indictment against me. Enclosed you will find an affidavit made by me in response to those charges. Also enclosed are several newspaper articles which directly relate to this affidavit and articles which cover the period of trial. You will note that I was acquitted on all these charges. Not shown in these articles or in the affidavit is the fact that I am a one-man company with a part time secretary. Not shown is the fact that my defense cost $72,000.00. Not shown is the fact that this money represents more than the total effort for thirteen years of business. Not shown and not included in the above figure are the six months that I was basically out of business preparing a defense against these charges.

I trust you will find this material of interest and I invite your comments.

Truly,

Martin L. Kaiser
President

MLK;nre
Encl.

Fifteen years after my acquittal, I again penned a letter to the grand jurors. Regrettably, the *worst advice* I have ever received in my entire life came from my best friend Kamal Sirageldeen. He suggested that I drop the issue and avoid sending this letter. I accepted his advice. Bad, bad, bad, *bad* decision.

Here is the letter I planned to send.

February 1994

An open letter to the Grand Jury members of 1978

Dear Sir or Madam:
February marks the 15th anniversary of my trial resulting from a criminal indictment handed down by you.

Shortly after that trial I wrote to all of you outlining certain facts and a rough cost of my efforts. A list of your fellow Grand Jurors is enclosed.

With this letter I will bring you up to date as to what has transpired since my acquittal. Enclosed find a series of articles and letters that adequately explain the general events. Not shown are the costs of legal fees and related expenses that came to about $285,000.00. This does NOT include the loss of business that resulted...which I estimate conservatively in the millions of dollars.

After my trial I was declared "persona-non-grata," or personally not welcome, by the entire intelligence community (if you wish to call them that). To this day I have not sold one single dime worth of equipment to that group of people. At the time of my trial my efforts were already shifting towards assisting bomb technicians. I have since built the same strong reputation there that you helped destroy elsewhere.

Please feel free, after all this is a "free" country, to contact me with any questions or comments. By the way, during the civil process I saw all 24 of the ORIGINAL letters I sent you initially. Also, I was able to read ALL Grand Jury testimony relating to the entire Northwestern Bank affair. SHAME ON YOU!!

Thank you for taking the time to review this information.

Truly,

Martin L. Kaiser, President
Martin L. Kaiser, Inc.

In early 1980, the British Broadcasting Company (BBC) contacted me and indicated they were doing a special about an individual I knew well, Frank Terpil. It was to be titled

Confessions of a Dangerous Man. I didn't realize what a pivotal role I played in the movie, but it was fascinating to do and see. My friend is still out there in the world somewhere, and I may expand on this story at a later time. The satisfaction I got out of it was being referred to as "a master craftsman with uncompromising honesty." The movie was banned from being shown in the United States. You may view it on my website.

CHAPTER ELEVEN

The Civil Case

Wasn't *this* an interesting turn of events.

The Daily Telegraph
London, England
Tuesday, January 2, 1979

Bugged FBI Men with Hemorrhoids
Sue for £11 Million (US$22,000,000)

A telephone tapping expert who supplied the Federal Bureau of Investigation with electronic eavesdropping devices is being sued for alleged "bugging of two FBI agents." The agents, Thomas Brereton and Zachary Lowe, are claiming eleven million pounds compensation They say their right as private citizens were "grossly violated" and they are suing Mr. Martin Kaiser and a bank in consent North Carolina.

They were investigating the bank's affairs after allegations that an executive was misusing funds, and according to Mr. Kaiser a vice president of the bank sought his assistance, wanting recorders installed to tape conversations and interviews in the bank involving the officers.

Devices were provided, Mr. Kaiser said, on the understanding that the equipment would be used legally with the of the agents.

The FBI men have now named him together with the bank in a lawsuit filed at Greensboro, North Carolina. In a court deposition Mr. Brereton tells of finding five bugging devices, including special transmitters and amplifiers, in the building.

He recalled: "That night there was tremendous anger and frustration". He remembered one of the bank's executives sitting "smirking at me when he pulled all the mikes out of the wall. He went on: "You wouldn't believe the anger that took place in here that night when I found out…you go home and all you do is think about it." "You know you've been bugged… It keeps playing on your mind".

As a result, he was humiliated and embarrassed as a special agent and suffered, he said, increased hypertension and cysts in his eyes.

His colleague said in his deposition that after the incident his hemorrhoid condition worsened.

———————————

Fraud n. the intentional use of deceit, a trick or some dishonest means to deprive another of his/her/its money, property or a legal right. A party who has lost something due to fraud is entitled to file a lawsuit for damages against the party acting fraudulently, and the damages may include punitive damages as a punishment or public example due to the malicious nature of the fraud. Quite often there are several persons involved in a scheme to commit fraud and each and all may be liable for the total damages. Inherent in fraud is an unjust advantage over another which injures that person or entity. It includes failing to point out a known mistake in a contract or other writing (such as a deed), or not revealing a fact which he/she has a *duty to communicate,* such as a survey which shows there are only 10 acres of land being purchased and not 20 as originally understood. Constructive fraud can be proved by a showing of breach of legal duty (like using the trust funds held for another in an investment in one's own business) without direct proof of fraud or fraudulent intent. Extrinsic fraud occurs when deceit is employed to keep someone from exercising a right, such as a fair trial, by hiding evidence or misleading the opposing party in a lawsuit. Since fraud is intended to employ dishonesty to deprive another of money, property or a right, it can also be a crime for which the fraudulent person(s) can be charged, tried and convicted. Borderline overreaching or taking advantage of another's naiveté involving smaller amounts is often overlooked by law enforcement, which suggests the victim seek a "civil remedy" (i.e., sue).

In short, it says fraud is using deceit or trickery to deprive another of his money. This is the part we all think of when someone uses the word *fraud.* The other, and most important, part of the definition is failure to speak when you have a duty to do so. I'll leave it up to you to decide whether the agents were duty bound to state they intended to sue after the criminal process was complete.

Fensterwald put forward an immediate response of abuse of power. His key motion was fought tooth and nail by the government and the FBI. In the end, the FBI was forced to give me *all* of my FBI files and the government *all* of the grand jury testimony.

Again, So Much For Grand Jury Secrecy!

My team and I traveled to North Carolina to receive and review the documents/files. To my amazement, right on top of the stack were *all twenty-four of my* original *letters to the grand jurors.* Once the shock of seeing those letters dissipated, my thoughts turned to anger. I thought, *Not one of those grand jurors had the guts to say to the FBI, "Hey look, this letter was sent to* me *and it is mine to keep."* The FBI must have frightened the hell out of them with a threat of criminal prosecution if they did not turn over the letters. I later learned that the US's attorney did indeed try to indict me for tampering with a grand jury but since my grand jury had long since been dismissed, that was a bunch of crap. Also, in those files were the *original* letters I had sent to several members of Congress and senators. With regard to those letters, all I can say is it was an exercise of pissing into the wind.

We also uncovered the fact that the two FBI agents asked for and received permission to sue me civilly *three months* before seeking my criminal indictment. There was absolutely *no* mention in the FBI files of *conflict of interest.* There was absolutely *no* mention in the thousands of pages of grand jury testimony covering all related defendants that the FBI agents intended to sue the defendants for a huge sum of money once convictions were obtained.

To me, this was absolutely horrible! The FBI destroyed my business after the U.S. Recording fiasco and they destroyed the Constitution of the United States to further punish me.

Where and when was this going to *stop?* That is when I decided that the price of freedom is not "free" and I was going to do my best to expose the FBI as the bunch of trash that they were/are. I couldn't help but notice the FBI files contained many, many green document sign-out slips. Actually, they approximated roughly one fifth or 20 percent of the total file. They were signed out by none other than one of the very FBI agents who was suing me for $22,000,000.00. In the end, we were *never* able to recover the files that had been removed. So, *this* is the FBI's definition of "fair play."

My team now plowed into the *thousands* of pages of grand jury testimony covering not only my case but those of Duncan, Starr, the EVP, and present and past employees of Northwestern Bank. We quickly learned that the grand jury was being run by FBI Agent XB and not the US attorney. Many of the statements made by the FBI agent were patently untrue. For example, he presented my countermeasure or de-bugging equipment catalog with the comment, "Here is Mr. Kaiser's catalog of illegal equipment." Absolutely *nothing* in that catalog was "illegal" and I could sell those products to whomever I wished, and I did—to Northwestern Bank.

Winston-Salem Journal (Sentinel) Friday, April 2, 1982

Bugging Expert Adds FBI To His Suit Against Agents By Mark Wright

Greensboro—A Maryland electronics expert is asking for more than $10 million in damages from the FBI, claiming that the agency assisted two of its agents who were planning a lawsuit against him.

Martin L. Kaiser, who specializes in electronic surveillance (bugging), countersurveillance and bomb-detection equipment says in a document filed in federal court here that agent Thomas J. Brereton and Zachary T. Lowe were contemplating a lawsuit against him while they were involved in prosecuting him on criminal charges.

The FBI "actually assisted and enabled...Brereton and Lowe to gain access to information and records while on bureau time and through bureau resources of information directly bearing to the outcome of their proposed civil action." Kaiser claims.

He says in the document, which is an amendment to an earlier counterclaim against the agents, that the FBI's action represents a "malicious motive for the institution and prosecution" of the criminal case against him "in violation of federal statutes which requires federal agents with a conflict of interest to recuse themselves from such investigation."

Brereton and Lowe sued Kaiser in U.S. Middle District Court in July 1978 five months after he was found not guilty of charges of bugging them while they were conducting an investigation at Northwestern Bank in Wilkesboro in 1977.

The agents also sued the bank and its former president, Edwin Duncan Jr., claiming that their right to privacy was violated by the bugging of the room they were using at the bank headquarters. The agents claim a total of $22 million in damages.

Several months later Kaiser filed a counterclaim against the agents, claiming they abused the criminal process against him and asking for $720,000 in damages. The agents responded by denying that they had acted improperly in the criminal investigation and they asked for a dismissal of the counterclaim.

Kaiser's addition to the counterclaim, filed this week asks that the United States be brought into the suit to represent the FBI and he asks for an additional $10.7 million in damages.

U.S. Attorney Kenneth W. McAllister said this morning that "I certainly wouldn't comment on any pending civil action."

Duncan and the bank have filed motions for dismissal of the agent's suit and Duncan has asked the court for permission to file his own counterclaim against the government and prosecutors in a 1977 criminal case against him.

Duncan pleaded guilty to charges of conspiring to bug the agents. He spent several months in prison as a result of the convictions on other charges stemming from the agents' investigation.

No trial dates have been set in the lawsuit, which has become one of the most complex civil cases now pending in the district.

The Sentinel
Winston-Salem, NC
Saturday, February 5, 1983
Defendants Claim Agents Abused Process

GREENSBORO, NC—Two FBI agents abused the criminal process to strengthen their position in a $22 million lawsuit stemming from the 1977 investigation and bugging at Northwestern Bank lawyers for defendants in the suit charged in federal court yesterday.

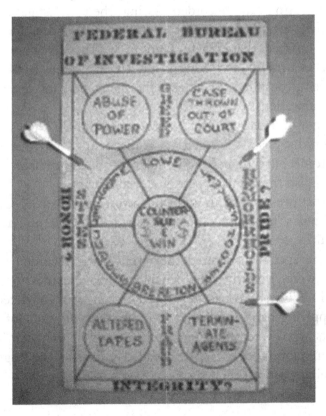

One defendant in the civil case also accused the FBI of tampering with evidence. In an affidavit, defendant Martin L. Kaiser, an Electronics expert from Cockeysville, MD., said bureau agents or employees altered two tape recordings and switched tape recorders. He also claimed that one agent removed documents from FBI files which have never been recovered.

The allegations were made during three hours of argument In U.S. Middle District Court Federal Judge Frank W. Bullock Jr. held a hearing on numerous motions pending in the case which began almost five years ago.

In July 1978, FBI agents Thomas J. Brereton and Zachary T. Lowe filed suit alleging that their civil rights were violated and their privacy was invaded when their conversations were electronically recorded during their investigation of Northwestern Bank from April to July 1977. Brereton and Lowe charged that Edwin Duncan Jr., then Northwestern Bank chairman, and Gwen E. Bowers, then bank vice president, conspired to intercept the agents oral and telephone communications.

They also claimed that Kaiser agreed to help Duncan and Bowers by possessing, selling, transporting, and installing electronic surveillance equipment or bugs to help them accomplish their sinister conspiratorial scheme."

Northwestern Bank and Northwestern Financial Corp., the bank's holding company, also are defendants in the lawsuit.

The agents discovered they were being recorded while they were investigating financial irregularities at the North Wilkesboro-based bank. Duncan was convicted of misapplying bank funds and recording conversations of IRS agents who were reviewing bank records in October 1977, and in November 1977, he pleaded guilty to the bugging conspiracy against the FBI.

Bowers pleaded guilty to the conspiracy to record the FBI agents' conversations and to the actual bugging. However, Kaiser pleaded not guilty to charges related to the bugging and he was acquitted in federal court in Winston-Salem in February 1978.

Since Brereton and Lowe's suit was filed, it has become one of the most complicated civil cases ever in the U.S. Middle District. Three Greensboro attorneys—Bynum N. Hunter, Michael R. Abel, and Ben F. Tennille, have been released as defendants, and the remaining defendants and the plaintiffs have filed pages and pages of motions' affidavits and cross claims. There also is a similar case filed by former FBI agent Donald G. Wilson for $5.5 million in damages from Duncan, Bowers, Northwestern Bank and Northwestern Financial.

Lawyers for Duncan and Kaiser yesterday said Brereton and Lowe used the criminal investigation of their clients to prepare for their multi-million-dollar civil suit. "They were given access and power of the federal government they should not have been given," Stephen Spring, a Louisiana attorney representing Kaiser said. Duncan's attorney, Ted G. West, claimed that the former bank chairman Agreed to plead guilty to the bugging conspiracy during a meeting with Brereton and a former U.S. attorney.

"We contend that Mr. Brereton and Mr. Lowe abused the process," West said. "That's what it boils down to in instigating a guilty plea from Mr. Duncan so they could have something to hang their hat on in this civil case."

He also said, "This court must and should look closely at a situation where investigators of the U.S. government pursue their investigation knowing during the entire course of the investigation that they have a civil suit in mind."

But Mike Bailey, one of Brereton's and Lowe's lawyers, said the agents were only fulfilling their obligations by investigating and helping prosecute the cases.

Kaiser filed a $720,000 counterclaim against Brereton and Lowe in 1978 and last year he asked to add the FBI to his suit. He is seeking $10.7 million from the FBI. Kaiser claimed the bureau "actually assisted and enabled...Brereton and Lowe to gain access to Information and records while on bureau time and through bureau resources of information directly bearing to the outcome of the civil action."

Duncan also has asked the court to allow him to add the FBI, a former U.S. attorney and a former assistant U.S. attorney to his cross-claim against Brereton and Lowe. However, Bullock questioned whether the statute of limitation on adding to the crossclaims has run out.

Kaiser made other allegations against the FBI in his affidavit. He accused the bureau of fraudulently concealing and manufacturing evidence.

The Panasonic tape recorder presented at his criminal trial played at one-third normal speed, Kaiser said, but he said the recorder being used as evidence in the civil case operated at one-fourth normal speed. He also said tests showed that two tape recordings of Brereton and Lowe were not made on the tape recorder provided to Northwestern Bank in 1977 and that the two tapes were made on two different recorders, he said.

Kaiser said, "It is my belief based upon a review of tests that these modifications or manufacturing of evidence was performed by agents and/or employees of the Federal Bureau of Investigation as part of a conspiracy wherein the FBI acted in concert with plaintiffs Brereton and Lowe by attempting to convict me of a crime I did not commit...and instituting the present civil suit as a retaliatory measure designed to drain me of funds necessarily spent in my defense."

Kaiser further charged that Brereton took documents out of the FBI files and that the bureau claims those papers are lost. He also said Brereton made misrepresentations to a grand jury which led to Kaiser's indictment on charges related to the bugging.

Brereton did that Kaiser said, so he could use the criminal trial to gather evidence for the civil case.

Duncan and Kaiser have filed motions for summary judgment and have asked for dismissal of the actions against them. Yesterday, attorneys for Northwestern Bank and Northwestern Financial Corp. also argued for summary judgment and dismissal.

"The bank was the one who was losing from this illegal activity" not just the customers, The bank," Richard Vanore, Northwestern attorney, said. "Because (Duncan) benefited is not sufficient to say the bank benefited and should be held responsible for his action."

He also charged that Brereton and Lowe are "seeking monetary damages as the real fruit of their criminal investigation"

It was now time to add the FBI to my lawsuit because of the overwhelming evidence of a massive conspiracy.

The Sentinel
Winston-Salem, NC
Friday April 2, 1982
Bugging Expert Adds FBI to His Suit Against Agents

GREENSBORO, NC—A Maryland electronics expert is asking for more than $10 million in damages from the FBI, claiming that the agency as assisted two of its agents who were planning a lawsuit against him.

Martin L. Kaiser specializes in electronic surveillance (bugging), Counter surveillance and bomb detection equipment says in a document filed in federal court here that agents Thomas J. Brereton and Zachary T. Lowe were contemplating a lawsuit against him while they were involved in prosecuting him on criminal charges.

The FBI "actually assisted and enabled...Brereton and Lowe to gain access to information and records while on bureau time and through bureau resources of information directly bearing to the outcome of their proposed civil action", Kaiser claims.

He says in the document which is an amendment to an earlier counterclaim against the agents, that the FBI's action represents a "malicious motive for the institution and prosecution" of the criminal case against him "in violation of federal statutes which require federal agents with a conflict of interest to excuse themselves from such investigation."

Brereton and Lowe sued Kaiser in U.S. Middle District Court in July 1978, five months after he was found not guilty of charges of bugging them while they were conducting an investigation at Northwestern Bank in Wilkesboro in 1977.

The agents also sued the bank and its former president Edwin Duncan Jr., claiming that their right to privacy was violated by the bugging of the room they were using at the bank headquarters. The agents claim a total of $22 million in damages.

Several months later Kaiser filed a counterclaim against the agents claiming they abused the criminal process against him and asking for $720,000 in damages. The agents responded by denying that they had acted improperly in the criminal investigation and they asked for a dismissal of the counterclaim.

Kaiser's addition to the counterclaims filed this week asks that the United States be brought into the suit to represent the FBI, and he asks for an additional $10.7 million in damages.

U.S. Attorney Kenneth W. McAllister said this morning that "I certainly wouldn't comment on any pending civil actions".

Duncan and the bank have filed motions for dismissal of the agents' suit, and Duncan has asked the court for permission to file his own counterclaim against the government and prosecutors in a 1977 criminal case against him.

Duncan pleaded guilty to charges of conspiring to bug the agents. He spent several months in prison as the result of convictions on other charges stemming from the agents investigation.

No trial dates have been set in the lawsuit, which has become one of the most complex civil cases now pending in the district.

Periodically, my anger would boil over and I would send off a letter or two expressing my displeasure with the treatment I was getting. Here are two of those letters.

MARTIN L. KAISER, INC.
Countersurveillance · Bomb Detection
· Surveillance Electronics

9 July 1983

The White House
Washington, D C 20500
Attention: Mr Ronald Reagan, President

My Dear Mr President:

You certainly had no difficulty understanding the seriousness of the potential conflict of interest concerning the Carter briefing books so I am at a loss to understand why you failed to see just as obvious a conflict as outlined to you in my letter of 15 February, 1983.

First, let me state that your response placed me right back in the hands of my enemies and you certainly get no thanks for that.

Let me again cite some of the events that have occurred in my action against some corrupt FBI agents.

During the civil process one of the agent/ plaintiffs revealed that they had been given my national security file. Check this out! Here I am fighting a corrupt group of FBI agents blindfolded, my hands tied behind my back, my cards being dealt face up and the bastards, in spite of that tremendous advantage, are dealing themselves from the bottom of the deck. No conflict, eh?

Every step of the way I have had to file subpoena after subpoena (at great expense) to obtain whatever material I needed to proceed with the case. When the FBI agent (the one with the sty in the eye) was pressed for an answer as to how many subpoenas he had issued for material in the case he responded "What do I have to worry...I'm the author. I know what's in those files...my God, I wrote 80 percent of everything in those files. I've done probably 60 percent of the work, and Mr Lowe (he's the one with the hemorrhoid) the rest of it...I know what's in the files. I wrote them."!!! No conflict of interest, eh?

Bullshit!

Truly,

Martin L Kaiser President

Encl:

P. O. BOX 171 · COCKEYSVILLE, MARYLAND 21030 · (301) 252-8810

MARTIN L. KAISER, INC.
Countersurveillance · Bomb Detection ·
Surveillance Electronics

27 July 1983
Federal Bureau of Investigation Washington,
DC 20535
Attention: William Webster, Director
Dear Mr Webster:

It seems ludicrous that I should be sending you a portion of the FBI manual of "Activities and Standards of Conduct" but since everyone else involved in the matter described in the attached article has forgotten about it I thought it best not to take any chances.

We now have a ruling from the Federal Court in North Carolina on my charges and they agree that your agents did indeed abuse <u>both</u> the criminal and civil process while acting under color of federal law. Granted they have the right of appeal but the issues raised fall within regulations covered by the manual of "Activities and Standards of Conduct."

I would like to call your attention to the following sections that I feel were violated by your agents. First, however, let me point out that the page enclosed is the first substantive one in the manual and is titled "Section 1" so I must conclude that someone must have thought these issues important.

1-1(1) The agents did not conduct themselves in such a manner that created respect for the Government.

1-1(3)(a) The agents did create the appearance of using public office for private gain.

1-(3)(d) The agents did create the appearance of losing complete independence or impartiality.

1-(3}(f} The agents did conduct themselves in such a manner as to adversely affect my confidence in the integrity of the Government.

The remainder of 1~1(3) concerns conflict of interest and is revealing.

1-2 The agents did engage in dishonest and disgraceful conduct which was prejudicial to the Government.

In view of the incredible expense and loss of business reputation these agents have put me through along with their causing me to lose my confidence in the integrity of the Government I am herewith demanding that they be summarily fired. I'm sure you can find a way to do this without interfering with the civil suit. After all it has been you all along that has said this is a purely private matter.

I shall press all issues raised by this case to conclusion by the court of law but it's up to you whether or not my confidence in government is restored.

Truly,

Martin L Kaiser President

Encl.
cc: President Reagan
Gerald McDowell

P. O. BOX 171 · COCKEYSVILLE, MARYLAND 21030 · (301) 252-8810

Here are the rules of conduct referred to in the above letter.

SECTION 1. ACTIVITIES AND STANDARDS OF CONDUCT

1-1 INTRODUCTION

Regulations concerning the conduct and activities of employees are published in the Code of Federal Regulations (CFR), Title 28, Section 45.735. Their source is found generally in Departmental Order 350-65 dated 12-28-65 which provides that employees shall:

(1) Conduct themselves in a manner that creates and maintains respect for the Department of Justice and the U.S. Government. In all their activities, personal and official, they should always be mindful of the high standards of behavior expected of them.

(2) Not give or in any way appear to give favored treatment or advantage to any member of the public, including former employees, who appear before the Department on their own behalf or on behalf of a nongovernmental person.

(3) Avoid any action which might result in, or create the appearance of—

(a) Using public office for private gain
(b) Giving preferential treatment to any person
(c) Losing complete independence or impartiality
(d) Making a Government decision outside official channels; or
(e) Affecting adversely the confidence of the public in the integrity of the Government

Departmental Order 350-65 further provides that an employee shall not have a direct or indirect financial interest that conflicts, or appears to conflict, with his Government duties and responsibilities. Such a conflict exists whenever the performance of the duties of an employee has or appears to have a direct and predictable effect upon a financial interest of such employee or of his spouse, minor child, partner, person, or organization with which he is associated or is negotiating for future employment. A conflict of interest is deemed to exist even though there is no reason to suppose that the employee will in fact resolve the conflict to his own personal advantage rather than to that of the Government. The order also provides that no Department of Justice employee shall participate personally and substantially as a Government employee, through decision, approval, disapproval, recommendation, the rendering of advice, investigation or otherwise, in a judicial or other proceeding, application, request for a ruling or other determination, contract, claim, in which, to his knowledge, he, his spouse, minor child, partner, organization in which he is serving as officer, director, trustee, partner, or employee, or any person or organization with whom he is negotiating or has any arrangement concerning prospective employment, has a financial interest, unless authorized to do so by the Deputy Attorney General. This prohibition includes such financial interests as ownership of securities of corporations or other entities which may become involved in Bureau investigation.

The prohibited actions include supervisory decisions and recommendations, as well as investigative activities. Any employee receiving an assignment involving any matters in which he has a direct or indirect financial interest as defined in the departmental order shall immediately advise his superior and shall be relieved of such assignment. Should there be a strong reason for requesting the Department's approval for the employee to participate in the assignment, the matter should be submitted to FBIHQ for consideration regarding presentation to the Department. In any event the employee should not participate in such assignment until the Department's authorization has been received. The departmental order specifically exempts from the above prohibition the stock, bond, or policy holdings of an employee in a mutual fund, investment company, bank, or insurance company which owns an interest in an entity involved in the matter provided the fair value of the employee's holding does not exceed one percent of the value of the reported assets of the mutual fund, investment company, or bank.

In furtherance of the above, the Bureau expects its employees to so comport themselves that their activities both on and off duty will not discredit either themselves or the Bureau. Copies of Departmental Order 350-65 are furnished to employees during their indoctrination on entering the Bureau's service. Failure by an employee to follow these regulations will result in appropriate disciplinary action including possible dismissal. The rules and regulations regarding official and personal conduct which govern the granting of individual access to and use of Bureau crypto materials appear in the COMSEC Custodian Manual (Section II, A, 5, pages 7-7c).

1-2 PERSONAL CONDUCT

Employees should never cause themselves to be mentally or physically unfit for duty. They are not permitted to consume alcoholic beverages during working hours, including that time allotted for meal periods or any period of leave taken if the employee intends to return to work before the termination of working hours. The use of illegal drugs or narcotics or the abuse of any drugs or narcotics is strictly prohibited at any time. They must not, at any time, engage in criminal, dishonest, immoral or disgraceful conduct or other conduct prejudicial to the Government.

1-3 GOVERNMENT PROPERTY

All Government property, automobiles, supplies, equipment, telephones, and facilities are to be used solely for official purposes and are not to be converted to any employee's personal use. In this regard, however, the use of equipment such as cameras for training and practice during non-work hours shall be considered "official purposes." Any loss, misplacement, theft or destruction of Government property issued to any employee must be reported to his superior immediately.

1-3.1 Bureau Vehicles

Bureau vehicles are to be used for official business only. In connection with the use of Bureau vehicles, transportation and related services for other than Bureau employees are to be restricted to individuals and their families, or aides accompanying them, who are traveling to attend Bureau sponsored or related functions or have other direct business to transact with Bureau officials and officials of the Department of Justice traveling on official business.

As mentioned earlier, *nowhere*, repeat *nowhere*, in the *thousands* of documents I reviewed did I find *any* mention of conflict of interest.

Repercussions

Here is a letter expressing my continuing frustration.

Martin L. Kaiser, Inc.
MANUFACTURER OF
SURVEILLANCE - COUNTERSURVEILLANCE -
BOMB DETECTION EQUIPMENT

29 November 1999

Immigration Board
Department of Immigration
P.O. Box 1098GT Grand
Cayman
Cayman Islands

Reference: 007956

Attention: Liz Walton
Secretary, Immigration Board

Dear Ms. Walton:

This letter is in response to yours of 10 September, 1999 to Mr. John Bostock of John D.Bostock Associates.

For the past 27 years (now 44 years) I have been a good citizen on the Cayman Islands and given generous financial and personal support to many, many charitable and civic organizations. On numerous I have assisted Royal Cayman Police Force in areas of my expertise. I sincerely regret the current state of affairs.

I place the blame for the destruction of my Cayman dream directly on the U.S. Federal Bureau of Investigation in particular and the U.S.

intelligence community in general. Allow me to explain.

Years ago your residency application asked "Have you ever been <u>charged</u> with a crime?" I would then have to say "Yes, I lawfully electronically bugged a couple of corrupt FBI agents." To express their displeasure they used the enormous power of the U.S. government to fabricate a crime, lie to a Grand Jury and falsely accuse me of committing that crime. They tampered with evidence they themselves had created and perjured themselves before the court. After I was acquitted they sued me for US$22,000,000.00 claiming I caused them mental anguish. One agent claimed I aggravated the sty in his eye and the other that I aggravated his hemorrhoids. That suit lasted for nearly ten years and cost me hundreds of thousands of dollars before it was dismissed. You may go to my web site and read more about this story. You may not agree with my methods but I tell you that the price of freedom is not "free."

Recently that same question on your residency application was changed to "Have you ever been <u>convicted</u> of a crime?" I immediately reapplied to immigration and answered "NO." Now, it appears, my actions were too late.

You have a beautiful Island…don't loose it. It is truly a pity that I shall not be part of it.

Respectfully,

Martin L. Kaiser
President
cc: Bostock Assoc.
U.S. Senator Barbara Mikulski (MD)

Martin L. Kaiser Inc.
MANUFACTURER OF SURVEILLANCE. COUNTER SURVEILLANCE. BOMB DETECTION EQUIPMENT

28 January 1999

The Honorable Barbara A. Mikulski
United states Senate
253 The World Trade Center
401 East Pratt Street
Baltimore, Maryland 21202

Subject: A matter of fairness

Dear Senator Mikulski:

Recently, Sandia National Laboratories received a grant to develop a disrupter.

A disrupter is a tool used by bomb technicians to disarm improvised explosive devices (IEDs) such as letter/mail, pipe or car bombs. Over the past 25 years I have sold hundreds of my disrupter to federal, state and local bomb squads.

The Federal Bureau of Investigation (FBI) then received a grant to purchase 400 disrupters of Sandia's design. What happened next is, to me, absolutely inconceivable. The FBI gave these disrupters away <u>free of charge</u> to virtually every bomb squad in the United States. My market went to <u>zero</u> overnight. Since my disrupter sells for roughly $4,000.00, the FBI's action meant an instantaneous loss of $1,600,000.00!

Martin L. Kaiser, Inc. consists a part-time assistance and myself. I'm sure you can appreciate that a loss of this magnitude is totally devastating to a company the size of mine. There is absolutely no way I can compete with the FBI.

159

When I telephoned your office and spoke with a member of your staff he told me to make sure I tell you exactly what help I wanted. Obviously, I would like you to help me recover from this loss. One solution would be to give the grant money directly to the bomb squads and allow them the option of choosing whatever disrupter is best for their needs. I would appreciate hearing any ideas you may have to resolve this dilemma. Your kind assistance and guidance will determine the future of my company.

Supporting documentation is available for your review. Please do not hesitate contacting me with any questions or comments. Until then, I remain,

Truly,

Martin L. Kaiser, President

P.O. BOX 171 · COCKEYSVILLE,
MARYLAND 21030 · U.S.A.
TEL: (410) 252-8810 . FAX: (410) 666-8790

United States Senate
Washington, D.C. 20510-2003

February 2, 1999
Mr. Martin L. Kaiser
President
Martin L. Kaiser, Inc.
P.O. Box 171
Cockeysville, Maryland 21030

Dear Mr. Kaiser:

Thank you for contacting me about the impact of the recent grant received by the Federal Bureau of

Investigation on your business. In response to your concern, I have requested that Mr. Louis J. Freeh, Federal Bureau of Investigation take a look at this issue. I have asked Mr. Freeh to respond to you directly. Thank you again for bringing this to my attention.

Sincerely,

Barbara A. Mikulski
United States Senator

Martin L. Kaiser, Inc.
MANUFACTURER OF SURVEILLANCE ·
COUNTER SURVEILLANCE · BOMB
DETECTION EQUIPMENT

16 February 1999

The Honorable Barbara A. Mikulski
United states Senate
253 The World Trade Center
401 East Pratt Street
Baltimore, Maryland 21202

Subject: A matter of fairness

Dear Senator Mikulski:

With reference to your response to my letter of 28 February...WHY THE HECK DID YOU DO THAT!? My God, Senator, it doesn't take a rocket scientist to figure out that Mr. Freeh is a COMPETITOR and he is using the enormous power of the United States Government to enforce that position. If any of his employees show up at my door to "investigate" this matter they are going to find themselves on the street sitting on their butts. I trust you would agree that this is the proper response.

Mr. Freeh obviously has no concept, whatsoever, of how the free enterprise system works and therefore cannot self-judge the damage he has caused. This matter should be placed in the hands of Attorney General Janet Reno. Would you be so kind as to assist in doing that? Please do not hesitate contacting me with any questions or comments. Until then, I remain,

Truly,

Martin L. Kaiser President

cc: sp sb

Never heard a word from Director Freeh.

The civil suit was finally settled in 1986. When my insurance company, Aetna, told me they were going to settle with the two agents, I became absolutely livid. I told them their course of action would destroy my civil suit against the FBI, a civil suit I had just spent roughly $250,000.00 (1986 dollars) on. They didn't give a flying damn. I subsequently had to drop my suit against the FBI, not because I was wrong but because I simply didn't have another million to throw away.

P.O. BOX 171 · COCKEYSVILLE,
MARYLAND 21030 ·
U.S.A.
TEL: (410) 252-8810 . FAX: (410) 666-8790

Martin L. Kaiser, Inc.
MANUFACTURER OF SURVEILLANCE ·
COUNTER SURVEILLANCE · BOMB
DETECTION EQUIPMENT

8 January 2001

The Honorable Barbara A. Mikulski
United states Senate
253 The World Trade Center
401 East Pratt Street
Baltimore, Maryland 21202

Subject: A matter of fairness

Dear Senator Mikulski:

Thank you for your continued assistance in resolving my problems with the FBI.

Once again, the FBI has unilaterally absolved itself of any wrongdoing. It is inconceivable they did this without ever interviewing the very person making serious accusations and holding the damning evidence.

I look forward to your response to my letter of 27 November 2000.

Respectfully,

Martin L. Kaiser
President

P.O. BOX 171 · COCKEYSVILLE,
MARYLAND 21030 · U.S.A.
TEL: (410) 252-8810 · FAX: (410) 666-8790

FBI AXIOM

If you lie in a court of law and get away with it, it is called "justice."

If you lie in a court of law and get caught, it is called "perjury."

Don't get caught!

CHAPTER TWELVE

From 1975 onward, I struggled to make a living and actually did fairly well under the circumstances. By 2005, the FBI had fully taken over the Bomb Data Center at Redstone Arsenal and the handwriting was on the wall for the bomb business. A few years after 9/11, the FBI had its act together and was throwing millions at just about any vendor who held their hand out. They bought hundreds of bomb suits and gave them away free to bomb squads. Med-Eng, the manufacturer of the bomb suit, decided they no longer needed a representative, so they fired me. The same with the manufacturer of the disrupter, the same with the manufacturer of the hook and line kit, and the same with many of the other vendors I represented. The "free enterprise system" took a real hit. That meant a substantial loss of income.

The harassment continued and continues to this day (2024). I made countermeasure equipment for the corporate market and bomb detection and disposal equipment for bomb squads worldwide. I continued to lecture as before, although when the FBI took over the Bomb Data Center in Huntsville, Alabama, I was *out*! I finally gave up on the Navy. I had lectured at both places for over twenty years without charging them a single dime.

I did a few movies. One was *Confessions of a Dangerous Man* (the Frank Terpil story) and another was *Enemy of the State* starring Gene Hackman and Will Smith. You may view the Frank Terpil story on my web site by going to http://www.martykaiser.com/sitema~1.htm and clicking on "My YouTube Movies." There are two other videos on that site that may interest you.

The idea for the movie *Enemy of the State* began shortly after the *Baltimore Sun* papers printed a six-part Sunday magazine article about the National Security Agency (NSA) a.k.a. No Such Agency. Walt Disney Productions/Touchstone Pictures saw the article and the potential for a movie, but felt that the NSA was one of those agencies that didn't attach to real people.

They put their research division into action and eventually found my website. Years ago, I had sold Disney one of my countermeasure kits. When Executive Director Andy Davis called, I assumed it was about the kit. We played phone tag for a while until we finally connected. Andy told me Disney wanted to incorporate *my FBI story* into the *Baltimore Sun* NSA story to make a movie. Sounded great. He invited me to California to meet with Jerry Bruckheimer. Bruckheimer sent the NSA articles and my FBI story to David Marconi, a British screenplay writer. Screenplays form the shell of the movie and must be no longer than 120 pages. David realized he would have to divide me into two different and distinct characters. One was the technical wizard (played by Gene Hackman) and the other was a victim of government abuse (played by Will Smith). Bruckheimer's writers and I took over from there and produced a script of over 2,500 triple-spaced pages. Hundreds more pages were added as the movie progressed.

By 2005, it was time to give serious thought to closing my business. I was unable to give myself a living wage and was existing on Social Security and income from my investments. I officially closed my doors in 2009 and sold my building. My "retirement" lasted about four months and I opened a new company making what I had made before and selling it on eBay. That made life a whole lot easier by getting rid of purchase orders and invoices. Here are two promo shots for *Confessions of a Dangerous Man*. Believe it or not, I knew where everything was on my workbench.

EPILOGUE

Ali Baba had it easy; he had only forty thieves to worry about. I had hundreds. The biggest single problem I faced during my fifty years in business was the rampant theft of my proprietary information, mostly by agents of the United States government.

When I first offered the 1080D telephone analyzer, I sold quite a few. One of those was to the F.G. Mason Company, manufacturer of the A2 countermeasure receiver. Mason's chief engineer, Sam Daskam, immediately set about copying the 1080D and did, in fact, copy it. His may have looked prettier but it was functionally the same as mine. Daskam went on to open his own company and he again made a copy of the 1080D telephone analyzer. He also copied the 1080H. Again, both were pretty but functionally the same. Lt. Col. Allan Bell also copied my telephone analyzer although rather than set selector switches for each test, his automatically stepped through each test. Each test interestingly represented one of the three by five flash cards I provided with my 1080D. I had a serious problem with Bell. He designed and built his analyzer while still in the military and that gave him essentially no overhead, engineering, and marketing expenses. Bell's analyzer also incorporated my 1080AVS vector oscilloscope. The CIA also made a copy of my analyzer. It is not in my best interest to describe the details of the theft but, again, it was functionally the same as the 1080D.

The 1059 audio preamplifier/amplifier also ran into competition from Lt. Col. Bell. He produced a product similar to the 1059 but used instead integrated circuits rather than discrete transistors. With one exception, they both worked exactly the same. I purposely used transistors rather than integrated circuits to make the 1059 easier to repair. If a transistor were to go bad, you simply had to buy a readily available transistor, stick it in, and you were back in business. The likelihood of finding a replacement integrated circuit in a foreign country in the 1970s was next to impossible.

An agent of the Bureau of Narcotics and Dangerous Drugs (BNDD, now the DEA) bought many of my products, like the SCD-5 carrier current detector, the 1059 audio preamp, and the 2050CA transmitter detector for cash. That did not seem unusual to me since FBI Special Agent Marion Wright was buying bugs for the FBI with petty cash funds. Again, the DEA agent had little or no overhead and ready marketing. What that agent forgot to tell me was that he had his own company that competed directly with mine.

In 1972, I first met CIA agent Glenn Whidden at the Pennsylvania State Police Academy in Hershey, Pennsylvania. Through his own company, he was offering several countermeasure products. Although I felt uncomfortable about directly competing with the United States government, it bothered me that he, like other former agents I had to deal with, was using information most likely sold to the government by companies like mine hoping to obtain more business. He retired from the CIA in 1974 and took with him information and knowledge that was not his to take. It also bothered me that he would receive a pension of roughly $40,000.00 per year and I would have to sell $120,000.00 of my products to get to that same financial position. The now former CIA agent Whidden would go on to open a countermeasure school.

Several firms copied my 2020N acoustical noise-masking device. A British firm copied the 2055HA nearfield detector.

The 7080 hostage negotiator was copied by a law enforcement agency employee, again while he was actively employed by the government. Another British firm copied my 2010A Doppler stethoscope. That one really hurt. His copy became standard equipment for every British bomb squad and I got zilch. The 2046I tape recorder detector was copied by three competitors. One competitor even went so far as to hire a private detective to steal my products.

I sold thirty-seven of my POW-GAL27 blasting machines to a California-based law enforcement supplier and he simply walked away from my invoice. I turned the account over to Dunn and Bradstreet, who collected the debt. To express his displeasure, he did what any red-blooded thief would do: he copied it.

Doms brought Dick Fink of Microtel Corporation to my plant to see my RAS515 raster analysis system. He immediately copied the product. Again, it looked prettier but was functionally the same.

There was a need for a radio frequency link between my 2049M and 2047U/C stethoscopes and a remote receiver. I made several modifications to the printed circuit boards and wiring to a commercially available wireless microphone. I received an order for six from an army EOD detachment. When I called them to see how they liked the unit and wondered if they wanted any more, the response was, "We can do that." So much for the free enterprise system.

People have asked me, "Why didn't you patent your products?" I have two patents and each cost roughly twenty thousand dollars. If you multiply that figure by one hundred products, you get two million dollars. The cost of litigating an infringement would add tens of thousands of dollars to protecting a patent. If, as in the case of Bell, Whidden, the DEA agent, and the CIA agent, I would also have had to sue the government agency they worked for, i.e., the U S Army, DEA, and CIA. That, I am sure you would agree, would be like throwing (pissing) money into a black hole. As a three-person company, there was no way I could burden those expenses.

Clarence Tuska, RCA's patent attorney, said that the "mere exercise of mechanical or electrical skills is not invention." I felt that what I built was an exercise in electrical skills, so basically a patent would not be deserved. At a Hackers of Planet Earth (HOPE) conference, a member of the audience asked about theft of my propriety information and my response surprised even me. I said, "I thought I was smart enough to develop new products faster than the old ones could be stolen." So, there you have it.

It has been an honor to know and work with many super-patriots like Frank Terpil, Marshall Soghoian, Bill Bhere, and Ed Duncan. They were truly remarkable.

Bill "Emil" Behre operated freely throughout Central and South America and Cuba. I enjoyed his many "war stories." He was responsible for the assignation of some really bad people. After his "retirement," Bill, his wife Sylvia, my friend Mary Oliver, and I roamed the countryside as the four amigos. We were the closest of friends. Added to the list were Mitch Werbel (manufacturer of the MAC10 machine pistol) and H. Leonard "Lenny" Berg. All were betrayed by the US government. For reason yet unknown, the US State Department under Henry Kissinger decided to shut down a goodly number of covert operations, including all of the above. Frank Terpil recently died in Cuba. Bill Behre was buried at sea by the US Navy. Marshall Soghoian was buried with honors at the National Cemetery in Arlington, Virginia. He was my source for documents received under the Freedom of Information Act (FOIA). Ed Duncan and Jerry Starr are buried in North Wilkesboro, North Carolina.

THE END

BIBLIOGRAPHY

Garrison, William Lloyd Garrison. "To the Public." Fair Use Repository. Accessed September 9, 2024, https://fair-use.org/the-liberator/1831/01/01/the-liberator-01-01.pdf.

Goodwillie, Susan. *Now Hear This: The Life of Hugh S. Knowles, Acoustical Engineer and Entrepreneur.* London, UK: Francis Press, 1999.

Panos, Lou. "Witness's Business Suddenly Drops." *The Baltimore Sun.* October 25, 1976.

Printed in the United States
by Baker & Taylor Publisher Services